"*Liberty to the Captives* is an extraordinary gift to the church. Ray Rivera has masterfully woven the biblical narrative with his years of incarnational ministry leadership. . . . Ray's keen insights empower both clergy and laity with the tools to fulfill their prophetic and pastoral call to engage the powers and set the captives free. This is a must-read!"

— GABRIEL SALGUERO
President, National Latino
Evangelical Coalition

"A journey of faith and theological reflection in the making of a man and his mission who is himself immersed in the urban context. Drawing from over four decades of ministerial experience in New York City, Raymond Rivera clearly and succinctly tells his story through the lens of biblical exposition, pastoral imagination, and practical application, which he weaves together to provide the church with a personal compendium for the task of doing ministry in captivity. . . . Anyone called to do ministry to the outcast, impoverished, and disenfranchised of the world (in effect, that's everyone) should read this book."

— LUIS CARLO
Associate Dean, Alliance Theological
Seminary, New York City

"As someone personally influenced and mentored by the life and ministry of Rev. Dr. Ray Rivera, I am excited that he's finally put his urban ministry wisdom on paper for all the world to read. . . . Rev. Ray has given us a book rich in personal narrative, biblical teaching, and practical wisdom with an urgent challenge."

— ELIZABETH D. RIOS
Executive Pastor, Save the Nations Church,
Fort Lauderdale

"Rev. Dr. Raymond Rivera has been called by many an intuitive and indigenous theologian, and his book bears witness to that assessment. His work is refreshing, exciting, and very much needed for those who envision a church that is engaged in the real world, particularly in urban centers throughout the United States."

— SAMUEL CRUZ
author of Masked Africanisms

Liberty to the Captives

OUR CALL TO MINISTER
IN A CAPTIVE WORLD

Raymond Rivera

With

José Carlos Montes

William B. Eerdmans Publishing Company

Grand Rapids, Michigan / Cambridge, U.K.

Published 2012 by
Wm. B. Eerdmans Publishing Co.
2140 Oak Industrial Drive N.E., Grand Rapids, Michigan 49505 /
P.O. Box 163, Cambridge CB3 9PU U.K.

Printed in the United States of America

17 16 15 14 13 12   7 6 5 4 3 2 1

ISBN 978-0-8028-6901-2

www.eerdmans.com

Dedicated to my wife Marilyn,
my children Susana, Esteban, Joel, Stacy, and Adam,
and my grandchildren

Contents

Foreword

I first heard Ray Rivera share his thoughts on captivity and liberation at a large conference hosted by the Christian Community Development Association a number of years ago. Hearing him speak with such passion about seeing people break free was exciting. I was struck then by how insightful his theology of captivity and vision for freedom were, and I am delighted that he has now written this book, which further unpacks his vision — a vision which, if we allow it, could have a profound impact on people of faith in this country. This is without doubt a prophetic word from a Christian voice fulfilling the genuine meaning of the word *prophetic.*

I have known Ray for many years and consider him not only a friend but also one of the most important voices of this generation. He is a leader whom many admire and have learned from, and whom many more should take note of. The work that he has been doing in New York City for almost fifty years has had a profound impact on the local communities in which he and others have tirelessly invested, and in addition, churches and communities around the world that have sought to model the holistic ministry that Ray has been preaching and living out in his own life have been transformed.

In his work, his activism, and his writing, Ray combines his years of experience on the streets of New York with a rigorous understanding of the Scriptures. He is a truly substantial theologian, a quality that must not be underestimated. But even more than that, he balances this with an unwavering commitment to his local community, which means that his theology stands up to the "street test." It is compelling because it is being so visibly and effectively worked out in the Bronx, in Brooklyn, and beyond.

Ray should be considered an elder statesman in the world of social justice. He has mentored thousands of pastors, activists, and faithful followers for many years — both directly and indirectly — and with the publication of *Liberty to the Captives*, a brand-new generation has the chance to benefit from his wisdom and experience.

But *Liberty to the Captives* is not simply words on a page. It almost feels like a living, breathing document, teaching and inspiring through well-known biblical stories that deal with the captivities we still find ourselves in today, offering hope of liberation and freedom to all.

Ray, in his usual pragmatic way, recognizes that we all find ourselves in the same captivity, although we may have grown up in different contexts and experienced life (both earthly and spiritual) in markedly different ways. To break out of this captivity into the freedom that Christ offered each and every one of us in his atoning sacrifice on the Cross, we all need to go about it in different ways. Ray insightfully suggests four paradigms for breaking out of captivity.

First, we might be called to engage our community, whether that is our church, local neighborhood, or racial or ethnic group. Another way of looking at this might be simply as "doing life together." We should readily and regularly affirm and walk with our brothers and sisters, generously give our time and resources, and most importantly, share our love. In these ways, we invite others to live in the freedom that we are experiencing, through restored relationships between each other and with God.

Sometimes, however, we must confront our communities, challenge the status quo, and prophetically call out those areas of life that are holding us back from living as a free and liberated people. We are called to be "salt and light," and if we can't do this in our own faith communities, we cannot hope to do the same in the world. We must not be afraid to be "Jeremiahs for our generation."

It is not only in our communities that we must seek change, however. As I have often written, and as Ray does in *Liberty to the Captives*, we must also confront the powers by working at a larger, structural level to bring about change and liberation from the captivity with which these systems often shackle us. As many of the biblical prophets, and many after them, did, we must hold the systems of our world up to the standards that God has set for us. Millions of people are caught in the captivity that "the pow-

ers" have perpetuated, including poverty in the midst of plenty and violence as the only means of resolving conflict. It is our job to expose these
injustices and offer the alternative vision that God has for his children.

But finally, we must also be ready to engage these same powers. Some
of the best known biblical characters provide examples of this. Both Daniel and Esther found themselves in systems that were hostile to them,
their people, and their beliefs. And yet, they were willing to put their lives
on the line and refuse to compromise, while also working within those
same systems. This is an affirmation and encouragement to all those
called into public service, that it is possible to work and engage from
within. Whatever others might say, a moral compromise is not always
necessary.

Ultimately, in this book, Ray is trying to challenge the captivity that
evangelicals find themselves in, a political and cultural captivity that limits how we can engage with our communities, our neighbors, and each
other. And he offers a radical and profoundly exciting vision of breaking
free of that captivity.

Ray Rivera is undeniably a leader in the Hispanic Evangelical community. But *Liberty to the Captives* is not a book just for Hispanic Christians. It
is a book that should be read by anyone and everyone. Fifty years of wisdom are packed into each page, as Ray provides numerous examples
from his life of bringing and nurturing that freedom he has been fighting
for every day of his ministry.

This is also a wonderful book about our theology. It will be read by
many in the academic world, and rightly so. But it is also a book for the
pews. At the heart of his argument is an affirmation (and challenge) that
we are all responsible to minister to our communities and to the powers
of this world. If we live into the life-giving truth of Christ's victory over
sin, we can play our part in building thriving communities, free from the
captivity of strife and squabbles, and in liberating the Kingdom of the
World for the Kingdom of God, so that *all* might find freedom and peace
in God.

Ray's ministry is a blessing to us all, and it is manifested clearly in the
pages of *Liberty to the Captives.* May it continue to bless all who read it for
years to come!

JIM WALLIS

Acknowledgments

◇✒◇

Many people have been traveling companions throughout my more than forty-five years of ministry. I am indebted to them, as I could not have achieved what I have without them. You will "meet" some of them within the pages of this book. These past four years, several people were involved in various capacities of the production of this book. In particular, Rev. José Carlos Montes, my spiritual son and student for more than twelve years, responded to God's call to be my partner on this journey of writing this book. He not only edited and re-edited this book numerous times, but also helped me to flesh out the theological concepts. He also contributed to enhancing and enriching them. His critique and insight organized and formatted the book by integrating my theology, historical context, and ministerial experience in such a way that it became a living document.

Other individuals who read the early manuscript and gave positive feedback include Elder Wanda Fontanez, Francisco Paco Lugoviña, Noemi Santana, Rev. Dr. Wilfredo Laboy, Bishop Ronald Bailey, and my wife Marilyn Calo Rivera. Rev. Juan Carlos Morales provided extensive feedback on content and theological concepts and contributed greatly to the references to writers and thinkers included in the footnotes. José's wife, Isabel Silva-Montes, also offered extensive edits and asked many questions that improved the text. Deacons Julio Rivera and Pedro Estevez gave much needed behind-the-scenes support. Also, my long-time assistant, Rosa Mercado, took care of all the administrative and communications tasks throughout the years.

Acknowledgments

I appreciate my friends and colleagues who contributed the endorsements you see in the back of the book. I extend heartfelt thanks to Rev. Jim Wallis of Sojourners, who wrote the book's foreword. He is a friend and peer of more than forty years who has influenced me greatly ever since the days of the Post-American. I especially thank Rev. Dr. Peter Heltzel of New York Theological Seminary and the Micah Institute, who spoke on my behalf to Bill Eerdmans and opened the doors for my book to be produced by Eerdmans Publishing.

At Eerdmans, I thank President Bill Eerdmans for meeting with me and allowing me to share my heart about the book. I'm so glad that he resonated with my purpose in writing this book. I hope I am as wise and healthy as he is when I reach his age. Andrew Hoogheem, my editor, was so helpful and in sync with me. He truly made my first editing process quite enjoyable and educational. Also, Linda Bieze, Jennifer Hoffman, and Victoria Fanning were instrumental in the editing, production, and publicity of the book.

Last but not least, I thank the leaders, members, and worshipers of the Sanctuary Church, and the board, staff, families, students, and participants of the Latino Pastoral Action Center and Family Life Academy Charter School. I appreciate their patience, prayers, and active encouragement during the production of this book. These past twenty years would not have been the same without them.

CHAPTER 1

Did You Know Our World Is in Captivity?

ᴍ

Have you ever looked at people and asked why there's such a difference between their intentions and actions — between what they say and what they do? When you look at the world around you, do you ever wonder how so much of it has gotten messed up? Families are falling apart. Marriages are failing. Kids are rebellious. More people are poor and needy. Systems and structures are not responsive to the needs of citizens.

Also, have you ever noticed that the usual solutions our society presents, like getting a good education or a good salary, often don't seem to do any good? People hone their intelligence only to figure out new ways to cheat the system. People use their gifts, talents, and wealth for their immediate families and friends, never noticing that some of their neighbors are starving or falling into physical, emotional, or chemical dependency.

As you try to make sense of why these things are happening, you may point to social problems, like materialism or the breakdown of family values. You might blame politics, pointing to the corruption and scandals in which our public officials are constantly being implicated. Or perhaps it's the state of the economy, the growing gap between the rich and poor. Then again, you might say it's cultural dynamics, all the biases and prejudices people have against each other. Or the problem is religion, the poor state of spirituality or corruption in religious institutions. Then again, you might believe that life is what it is, and we just have to deal with it. Or you might not have a clue what's going on.

Each of these reasons has elements of truth to it, but I sum up the totality of our human dilemmas in one word: *captivity!*

Captivity is a state of separation from God and bondage to self, the result of our sinful nature. Too often, we fail to understand God's plan for our lives, or we simply reject his call to be instruments of liberation and restoration for the people, institutions, and systems and structures in our society. This is why I have agreed to be God's messenger and have written this book. Someone has to proclaim this message clearly and unapologetically, with an appropriate sense of urgency, and a measure of conviction and humility. The world is in a state of captivity! At the same time, be encouraged that, through his inspired Word, the Holy Bible, God has granted us a blueprint for being free in the midst of captivity! Indeed, the Scriptures provide countless accounts and lessons that can guide us in playing an active role in God's liberating plan for our society.

Thankfully, God has a remedy for captivity, and he has called me to deliver this message to his creation — both in word and deed. And it is with this revelation that I have been one of God's instruments for nearly five decades. God's truth has given me the clarity and strength to be a catalyst for personal and social change. As he continues to call his people to action, he is using me to present the vital message that you need to *act* on your call both faithfully and courageously. This acting on your call is what I consider to be *ministry.*

Of course, you may be thinking, *I'm a longtime Christian and I'm already active in ministry through my church (or through some other parachurch, faith-based, or community-based organization, or through a business, school, or government agency). What does captivity have to do with me?* Or maybe you're a new Christian and have had little to no experience in ministry. You may be wondering why God would want you to do something about our captive world: *Even if he did call me, what could I possibly do? And how and where would I even do it? Besides, don't churches have pastors, elders, and deacons? Shouldn't I just leave this stuff to the professionals?*

Whichever one describes you, this book could prove to be a godsend! For one, it will help clarify your calling and even teach you to minister, or serve, in situations of captivity. It also will help you identify your call and equip you to minister in captivity. For these reasons, I ask you to join me in this journey. As I share experiences and insights from nearly five decades of ministry, you will learn about captivity and how to minister in situations of captivity. You will discover how we live in a world full of fallen people and systems that are crying out in their pain. In the process,

2

you will learn how to bring forth hope and redemption to the people around you. Along the way, you will be in constant dialogue with God, and you will even see God in yourself.

Within these pages, you will meet people from the Bible and from our own time who have both virtues and flaws. You will find that their callings, convictions, and even confusions became fertile ground for God's divine activity in the midst of captivity. Indeed, every generation has produced instruments of God who have ministered in the midst of captivity. I pray that, with the help of this book, you will be counted as one of this generation's examples. I also pray that you will interact with the world around you, navigating the relationships within and outside your community, and working within and outside the systems and structures of our society.

As you read this book, you can embrace the fact that God has freed you to minister in our captive world. You can accept your God-given call to minister in captivity. You also can learn how to apply the four ways, or paradigms, of ministering in captivity that I will describe. In the chapters that follow, I will describe these paradigms, offering historical context and biblical/theological backgrounds, as well as examples from my more than forty-five years of ministry. In the next chapter, I will share several considerations as you minister in captivity. All throughout, you can learn from countless examples from the Scriptures that I will include, which will enable you to "test the spirits" (1 John 4:1).

Before I go on, you should know two of my presuppositions, or basic beliefs. First, I view the Holy Bible as the inspired Word of God. Christians have all kinds of different ways of reading and interpreting the Bible, be it symbolically, figuratively, or metaphorically. But I learn God's intention and instruction for his creation through the Bible. I find comfort and direction from the accounts and lessons of the Old and New Testaments. I also understand today's captivity through its pages. Naturally, the Holy Spirit helps me gain insights from it.

Second, although I understand that our final resting place is the afterlife, I believe we are called to focus on God's Kingdom here on earth: "Your kingdom come, your will be done in earth, as it is in heaven" (Matthew 6:10). As we await the return of our Lord and Savior, we have been empowered to do greater things in the Spirit than he did: "He who believes in me, the works that I do he will do also; and greater works than these he will do, because I go to my Father" (John 14:12). It is with this knowledge that I pray you will be inspired and better prepared to proclaim liberty to the captives. And I pray that, as a result, you will be able to engage others in shaping a world that meets the needs of others and reflects the shalom (Hebrew word for peace) of God.

CHAPTER 2

But You Are Free to Minister in Captivity!

⌒*ψ*⌒

S o what does it mean that our world is in a state of captivity? Can we really be free in the midst of captivity?[1] I invite you to join me as we journey through God's Word to discover the answers to these and other questions. Along the way, you will learn how God set the perfect example for ministry. You will recognize how humankind brought about captivity, or separation from God. You also will appreciate how Christ freed us from captivity so we can minister in the midst of our captive world.

---

1. My concept of captivity first came to me after learning about Rev. Dr. Orlando Costas — pastor, missiologist, missionary to Latin America, theologian, professor, and author. His idea of the cosmological fall being all-encompassing influenced my theological understanding. I was already doing ministry, but I was fascinated and challenged by the fact that a Christian evangelical theologian was speaking about social-political-economic-cultural issues from a biblical perspective. Prior to that, I had relied on the cultural and political literature to give me a perspective on these matters. Afterward, I understood that the evangel no longer spoke just to the personal. It involved the whole gospel to the whole person and the whole world. The books by Costas that impacted me were as follows: *Christ Outside the Gate: Mission Beyond Christendom* (Maryknoll, NY: Orbis Books, 1982); *The Church and Its Mission: A Shattering Critique from the Third World* (Wheaton, IL: Tyndale House, 1974); and *Theology of the Crossroads in Contemporary Latin America: Missiology in Mainline Protestantism, 1969-1974* (Amsterdam: Editions Rodopi, 1976). I also was influenced by Gustavo Gutiérrez and his concept of institutional sin, and the implications of faith on politics. The books that impacted me most were the following: *We Drink from Our Own Wells: The Spiritual Journey of a People* (Maryknoll, NY: Orbis Books, 1984); and *A Theology of Liberation: History, Politics, and Salvation* (Maryknoll, NY: Orbis Books, 1988).

Perhaps you've read the story before, but you probably have not heard it quite this way.

That's why I ask you to be open-minded. Perhaps you're the intellectual type, who reads with her mind. Or maybe you're the spiritual type, who reads with his heart. For this story, I'm asking you to read with both your heart and mind. Yes, learn the biblical basis for captivity. Also, recognize implications of captivity in today's society. But be sure to go further. Allow the Holy Spirit to take you through a path of self-discovery. Let him reveal your purpose. Invite him to guide you into all truth. Indeed, you can bring liberty to the captives!

God Created the Perfect Conditions for Ministry

The book of Genesis reveals that, from the beginning, God provided the perfect example for us to work, or serve, in a godly way:

> The earth was without form, and void, and darkness was on the face of the deep. And the Spirit of God was hovering over the face of the waters. Then God said, "Let there be light," and there was light. And God saw the light, that it was good. (Genesis 1:2-4a)

In the midst of chaos and darkness, God created for six days and established the basis for goodness. Each day, he assessed (1:2), planned (1:3a), implemented (1:3b), and evaluated (1:4a). On the seventh day, the Sabbath, he rested (2:2-3). These verses describe God's creative process — and they also provide a blueprint that enables us to reflect his goodness. Thus, in the darkness and chaos around us, we can bring light to the afflicted and the needy as Jesus calls us to do, even in the face of official disapproval (e.g., Mark 1:21-39).

Genesis also reveals that, on the sixth day, God made man and woman in his own image, after his likeness (Genesis 1:26-27). As a result, man and woman exhibited God-like characteristics, which reflected their true righteousness and holiness (Ephesians 4:24). Here is a summary of those traits:

- *Spiritual:* They communicated fully with God — as God spoke with man and woman, who heard and spoke directly with God (Genesis 1:28-30; 2:23; 3:9-12).

- *Emotional:* They cherished communion and companionship — as man received woman from God to be a companion, or helper (2:18, 20-23).
- *Mental:* They used their intellect — as man named the animals and plants and recognized God's work in creating woman (2:10, 23).
- *Physical:* They worked the land and kept it — as man worked without exertion or feeling that he was laboring (2:15), and then rested after working (2:3).
- *Social:* They engaged in relationships with God, other humans, and nature — as man and woman related to God, one another, and the garden (2:16, 23; 1:29-30).

Indeed, God also placed man and woman in an environment that was conducive for them to live and serve perfectly. Thus, both man and woman had fertile ground and a companion-helper (1:29; 2:18). They had the means to cultivate the land without having to experience labor (2:15). They also were made aware of the existence of evil, for the potential for captivity exists even in spaces where human beings can realize growth: "Of every tree of the garden you may freely eat; but of the tree of the knowledge of good and evil you shall not eat" (2:16-17a). And they knew the consequences for disobeying God: "for in the day that you eat of it you shall surely die" (2:17b). Thus, their obedience to God's specific appeal would enable them to avoid captivity to sin and death.

Humankind Brought about Its Captivity

Of course, you know what happened next. Man and woman disobeyed God's revealed will!

> So when the woman saw that the tree was good for food, that it was pleasant to the eyes, and a tree desirable to make one wise, she took of its fruit and ate. She also gave some to her husband with her, and he ate. (Genesis 3:6)

Thus, man and woman brought about their Fall, which ended their perfect communion with God. In turn, the Fall (of man and woman) released death into creation. Thereafter, death would become the enemy that all creation would fear. Everything in existence has been dying ever since. For this reason, God excluded Adam and Eve from the garden so they would not eat from the Tree of Life and live under an eternal curse. That way, Adam and Eve would be able to die with God's promise of redemption (3:15).

Indeed, the Fall began human history independent of God:

> Therefore the Lord God sent him out from the garden of Eden to till the ground from which he was taken. So he drove out the man, and he placed cherubim at the east of the garden of Eden, and a flaming sword which turned every way, to guard the way to the tree of life. (Genesis 3:23-24)

Man and woman entered a harsh world, having been condemned to a life of hard labor and sorrow (3:17-19, 22). They lost the direct presence of God and faced sin and depravity. No longer able to relate directly to God as they did in Eden, they now had to use their conscience, independent will, and imagination to communicate with God. In the process, they became self-aware and gained conscience, which introduced responsibility and guilt (3:9-10). It was the beginning of self-knowledge — the end of innocence and original righteousness.

Certainly, the Fall was a cosmic event. It encompassed not just humanity, but all human structures and systems as well (3:14-18). It permeated all of life, affecting all living things (Romans 8:22-23; Exodus 34:7; Deuteronomy 28:15). It irreparably altered man and woman's relationships with God (what we can call their upward journey). Thus, they hid and argued (Genesis 3:8-13, 16, 22-24). It irreparably altered their relationship with others and the environment (their outward journey). Thus, they had conflict and engaged in finger-pointing (Genesis 3:12, 16, 17). They also had to endure a harsh environment and experienced harsh labor (Genesis 3:13, 17-18).

Furthermore, it irreparably altered their relationship with themselves (their inward journey). Thus, they experienced fear and shame (Genesis 3:7, 10). Nevertheless, God revealed how he would redeem humankind and its fallen relationships (Genesis 3:15), which he promised through the holy offspring of his disobedient creatures. Indeed, Jesus Christ, the Son of God, ultimately would perform the perfect atonement that would reconcile us to God forever.

The Fall also altered divinely established systems and structures (Genesis 3:8, 16, 19). They no longer functioned perfectly as they did during Creation. They deteriorated into maintaining the nature man and woman acquired through their disobedience, not from God's transcendent vision. They no longer sought God's perfect communion. Subsequently, they sought to preserve the status quo, instead of being instruments of glorifying God.

For example, the institution of marriage, exemplified by companionship during Creation, gave way to man ruling over woman (Genesis 3:16). As for their schooling, whereas God had been their headmaster, man and woman now knew good and evil outside of God's teaching (3:1-6, 22). In the spiritual arena, they were expelled from the permanent dedicated space for their spiritual growth (3:23-24). Concerning civic life, the established healthy norms morphed into a system of laws that dished out punishment for violating them (3:14-19). Thus, work became hard labor (3:19), and environmental preservation gave way to exploitation, causing irreparable damage (3:18).

So just what did the Fall produce? *Captivity!* Captivity is a state of separation from God and bondage to self. Man and woman lost their true identity — their relationship to God. They also were separated from themselves, others, and the environment. In this state of separation, they began to seek meaning outside their relationship with God. They forfeited their creative purpose. They were bound to, and by, external forces. They no longer ruled, but were ruled over. They also began to experience suffering, abuse, oppression, betrayal, discrimination, deception, rejection, loss, and death.

The relationships of man and woman became epitomized by subordination and power. Hence, "Cain killed Abel" (Genesis 4:8). Also, man and woman sought to feed and submit to their carnal nature. They succumbed to the will of Satan (John 8:44; 2 Timothy 2:26).Their survival and self-preservation became paramount: After being judged by God for murdering his brother, Cain's first thought was for his own safety: "Anyone who finds me will kill me" (4:14). God showed mercy on Cain and protected him, but later he grieved so much over humanity's evil that he declared how sorry he was for creating them (6:7).

Indeed, captivity seeped into the totality of human existence, encompassing the social, economic, political, and spiritual realms. Abusers, adulterers, thieves, murderers, dictators, and terrorists are easy to point out. But captivity surrounds us everywhere we go. It is present in our families, churches, and schools. It permeates our workplaces. It has a seat at the boardrooms of businesses and corporations. Even the community-based organization across the street, with all the good it does, is not exempt from captivity. It is present in our foster care system and other social safety nets. It certainly permeates every level of government. It affects our healthcare and welfare systems. Our military and prison complexes cannot escape it either. Nothing exists or is produced without being impacted by captivity.

Captivity Is Brutal and Dehumanizing

Captivity strips people of their dignity and intrinsic self-worth. There's nothing glamorous about being stripped of self-respect, about being robbed of self-value. People hurt when they cannot make their own decisions for themselves and their loved ones. They cry out when they become objects of the prevailing powers. In the midst of captivity, people often encounter brutality and dehumanization, which is driven by Satan the murderer, destroyer, and devourer (John 8:44; 10:10; 1 Peter 5:8). Consequently, violence becomes the prevailing societal reality (Genesis 4:23-24; 6:11).

After the Fall, human beings were wicked and corrupt (Genesis 6:12). They blamed others (3:12-13); they deceived others (4:9). They disregarded and disdained life, even to the point of committing murder (4:8). They committed sexual abuse (34:1-2) and incest (19:30-38). They also became fugitives and wanderers (4:14). They experienced poverty (Exodus 1:11). They also experienced indentured servitude (Genesis 16:1-6) and imprisonment (39:20, 22).

Not surprisingly, people and institutions have encountered fierce opposition from systems and structures that no longer function according to their original purpose. In captivity, they are susceptible to and, at times, controlled by Satan, who exercises dominion and rule through laws and deep-set traditions (2 Corinthians 4:4; Ephesians 2:2). When this happens, they become principalities and powers (Ephesians 6:12). In fact, regardless of the ideology around which they organize (capitalism, socialism, or some other), they deteriorate this way. Thus, people and nations can be oppressive (Genesis 12:10-15). They commit genocide (Esther 3:8-11). They discriminate against the poor and sick (Isaiah 3:14-15). They engage in war (Genesis 14:1-2), enslave others (Genesis 37:26-28), and exploit others economically (Exodus 1:8-14). Even religious authorities become spiritually abusive and corrupt (Genesis 32:21-34).

Unfortunately, examples of brutality and dehumanization abound!

Children and adults lack affordable healthcare and are becoming sicker. An increasing number of the world's poor are experiencing high child mortality and cannot afford the out-of-reach prices for basic food staples. Many families cannot afford housing and have fallen victim to predatory and deceitful lending practices. Students are attending failing public schools. Workers have to receive public assistance because their employers refuse to provide living wages or health care. Children, women, and the poor are being thrust into drug and sex trafficking. Women are largely excluded from corporate decision-making roles, and most are paid less than their male counterparts.

In addition, African Americans, Latinos, and poor whites are filling our prisons. Immigrants are being forced to leave their homelands and arrive at the shores of the global economic powers that are enacting devastating global and local economic policies. Countless people are receiving unhelpful and disrespectful assistance from government and other public agencies. Community residents are receiving substandard services from community-based and other service organizations, and some who live near houses of worship are being denied service because they are not "card-carrying" members.

Captivity Has Led to Spiritual Decay

Captivity has caused us to seek the desires of the flesh — and not those of the Spirit. The spiritual sensitivities of man and woman have been anesthetized, which makes it difficult to hear God consistently and effectively. Thus, we must rely on indirect means to communicate with God. Yes, God spoke directly to Abraham (Genesis 12:1-2), Hagar (16:8-10), Moses (Exodus 3:4-6), Isaiah (Isaiah 6:8), Jeremiah (Jeremiah 1–2), Jesus' mother Mary (Luke 1:22-37), and Saul of Tarsus (Acts 9:4-6). But they were the exceptions, not the rule. In our day, we must rely on the Holy Bible and the Holy Spirit. Unfortunately, many listen to people and things other than God. They seek answers from science and from society, but do not seek answers from God.

This spiritual decay has resulted in broken relationships, which manifest themselves in many ways. Divorces now outnumber marriages — even among Christians. Physical and sexual abuse, even within families, is occurring at alarming rates. Child slavery and prostitution are fueling the economy of some nations. Numerous issues plague our relationship with our environment — climate change, our overreliance on fossil fuels, a decreasing number of available sites for garbage removal, our overuse of non-biodegradable products, even the increasing scarcity of fresh water — and our businesses and legislative bodies often try to deny there is a problem.

Captivity Has Led to Civic Decay

Needless to say, captivity has caused people, institutions, systems and structures, nations, and societies to function contrary to their intended purpose. Even God's people at times have failed to be light and salt in the world. Many do not engage or confront the powers or their own communities. They do not stand up to abusive and oppressive powers. They do not recognize the intrinsic value of strategically collaborating with the powers, or participating in civil service.

Many churches fail to equip the saints — that is, their members — opting instead to focus only on the clergy, elders, and deacons. Even when they do equip the laity, they focus on developing a few individuals rather than the collective. They fail to grasp that equipping both clergy and laity is necessary to bring about the godly prosperity, or shalom, they seek. Also, many churches fail to involve youth and women in leadership. In effect, God's people have been slow to discern and respond to God's movement for peace and justice. Consequently, people and institutions do not reach their God-given potential, purpose, or destiny.

In fact, we continue to see many of the same sinful atrocities as were perpetrated under the ancient empires of Egypt, Assyria, Israel, Judah, Babylon, Persia, and Rome. Like them, today's nation-states reflect the opposite of Kingdom values. They reject the renewal, reformation, and revolution expressed in the Lord's Prayer: "Your kingdom come, your will be done on earth as it is in heaven" (Matthew 6:10). And though we know of their corrupt acts, we accept them as distant, almost fictional accounts. Some individuals even argue that their lack of direct involvement in atrocities like war or genocide actually frees them from any personal or social responsibility. Not surprisingly, they turned a blind eye to Native Americans in the United States, Jews in Nazi Germany and the Soviet Union, the killing fields in Cambodia, Tutsis in Rwanda, Muslims and Croats in Bosnia, and non-Arabs in Darfur.

One glaring example of this is the implementation of local and global policies that have led to repression of ethnic groups, nations, and geographic regions (women working in *maquila* factories in Mexico, the worldwide sex-trafficking trade, indigenous laborers in Guatemala, and so on). These acts have been perpetrated throughout human history and continue today. You or your people may not have experienced them personally, but they are real all the same: Indentured servitude. Slavery. Forced migration. Internment and concentration camps. The takeover of independent nations. Terrorist attacks. And so many more. What's more, they may have been carried out by nations that once were under oppressive systems and structures themselves. Indeed, the oppressed often become the oppressors!

You also see it in our society's trust in militarism to secure and acquire territory and resolve conflicts. Yet, the biblical narrative reveals that whenever nations relied on their military strength, they eventually fell. They were triumphant only when their trust was in God. Some of these militaristic empires did last a long time, but each one eventually failed. Their horses and chariots simply were not enough. Not surprisingly, in the fully consummated Kingdom, militarism is absent (Isaiah 2:4). Instead, the nations walk in the light of the glory of God, and the kings of the earth bring their glory into it (Revelation 21:22-24).

Captivity Has Led to Dual Citizenship

As we await Christ's return, we live as dual citizens of the Kingdom of God and kingdom of man; nevertheless, the Kingdom of God is our primary citizenship.[2] Jesus said,

> I have given them your word; and the world has hated them because they are not of the world, just as I am not of the world. I do not pray that you should take them out of the world, but that you should keep them from the evil one. (John 17:14, 15)

Not surprisingly, you feel tension as a dual citizen. Like Moses, who by birth was a Hebrew but grew up an Egyptian, you may belong to a bio-

---

2. W. E. B. Du Bois addresses the issue of dual citizenship in *The Souls of Black Folk* (1903; New York: Penguin Classics, 1996).

logical or spiritual community that is oppressed, but then grow up with those who oppress you or your community.

At times, we are faced with the question of whether we will identify with a dominant culture that often is controlled by collective sin and collective principalities and powers, or whether we will side with the most vulnerable, suffering "least of these" in our midst — who may have issues related to the personal manifestations of sin in their lives, but still are victims of systemic sin. For me, I ask myself: *Will I align myself with my spiritual nature by defending the "least of these," or will I align myself with my carnal nature and ignore the suffering as I benefit from systems of sin? Will I allow myself to be reached by the redemptive restorative mission of God, or will I be in perpetual rebellion toward him?*

Regrettably, captivity has resulted in countless Christians adopting and applying worldly practices instead of modeling Kingdom values. We deny Christ's Kingdom mandate to feed the hungry, quench the thirsty, welcome the stranger, clothe the naked, and visit the sick and imprisoned (Matthew 25:35-36). We divorce as much as non-Christians. We perpetrate unfair lending practices and redline communities. We have shown partiality by embracing different standards for the rich and poor. Through our elected leaders, we have installed and financed known murderous dictators. At times, we have waged unprovoked wars. We even have commodified basic food staples around the earth, such as drinkable water, which has caused water scarcity around the world, especially in poor countries. In effect, too many have placed the oppressive values of the kingdom of man over those of the Kingdom of God.

Christ Freed Us from Captivity

Now, you might be thinking: *What do you expect from me regarding captivity? In fact, why should I even bother with this captive world and the captive people in it? And even if I wanted to do something, how can I possibly address the harm that humanity has caused itself and the world? Does anyone really have the means to reverse the consequences of our sins? In fact, when will the crying stop? When will all the needless death cease? Will we always have to mourn? And how will all the pain end?*

Indeed, to dwell on these and other discouraging questions could make even the greatest optimist spiral into a crippling state of cynicism. And if the answers to these questions were fully up to you, you would have good reason to sink into despair. Because of this kind of despair, people slip into escapism. They become dependent on drugs and alcohol, or indulge their sexual appetites and perversions, or seek an alternative "reality" in television and movies! On the other hand, this despair can lead people to adopt religious dogmatism, putting God in a box to avoid facing the reality of these tough questions. Or again, they turn to philosophies like secular humanism, in which God is not even in the picture, or to nebulous "New Age" spiritualities in which God is essentially whatever they want him to be!

Fortunately for us all, God has the response to these issues! In the midst of captivity, he offers the possibility and potential for redemptive change. He has called all of his creation to be agents of liberation and transformation for people and systems, both as individuals and as groups. He has used animals — even a donkey (Numbers 22:28), an ant (Proverbs 30:25), and a worm (Jonah 4:7). He also has used the stars and moon (Psalm 8:3). He also has invited and called *you* to participate with him to accomplish his purpose. Toward this end, he provides resources and participates in human history so you can succeed in your call.

In Jesus Christ, God brought about our redemption from the death ushered in by the individual and collective sins committed by man and woman. His work on the cross represented the payment for the debt we owed God because of our sins, and through that work we received eternal redemption. He became the curse, delivering us from our curse (Galatians 3:13, 14). He enabled us to benefit from God's promise of blessing all humankind (Genesis 12:13). Thereafter, God saw those who accepted Christ as Lord and Savior through Christ's blood (Romans 5:9; 10:9-13). Christ's righteousness became our righteousness (2 Corinthians 5:21).

Christ's act was a permanent atoning sacrifice that paid our debt in full (John 3:16; Romans 3:25; Ephesians 1:7; 1 Peter 1:18-19). He alone redeemed us from the slavery of sin (Psalm 130:7-8) and the power of death (Job 19:25-26; Psalm 49:8, 9). He also saved us from the wrath of God (John 8:34; Romans 6:18; Hebrews 2:14-15). Thus we were reconciled, adopted, sanctified, and ultimately will be glorified (Romans 8:29-30). Our bodies were redeemed (Acts 3:19; 26:18; Romans 8:15-23; 1 Corinthians 15:55-57; Ephesians 1:7; 2 Timothy 2:26; Hebrews 2:9), and our souls moved toward a larger and fuller life (John 10:10-11). God also ensured our return to the privilege of having dominion over the earth (Genesis 1:28; Revelation 5:9-10).

Through Christ's work of redemption, we achieved personal freedom:

Christ redeemed us from the curse of the law by becoming a curse for us — for it is written, "Cursed is everyone who is hanged on a tree" — so that in Christ Jesus the blessing of Abraham might come to the Gentiles, so that we might receive the promised Spirit through faith. (Galatians 3:13-14)

Thus, we no longer are subject to the dominion and curse of sin (1 Corinthians 15:56), or the law (Galatians 4:3-5; 5:1). We no longer are under bondage to Satan, the ruler of darkness, or even to death (Acts 26:18; Hebrews 2:14-15). We, who freely seek to be saved in Christ (John 14:16; 2 Peter 1:11), experience eternal life (Matthew 19:16, 17; John 3:15), abundant life (Deuteronomy 30:15, 16), and interdependent life (Acts 2:42-47; 4:32; Ephesians 4:1-6; Hebrews 2:14-15; 10:25; 2 Peter 1:3-7). We also achieve structural freedom, which allows us to transcend our social, religious, national, and ethnic conditioning. Moreover, we can discern the spiritual dimensions behind the systems (Matthew 4:8-10).

Through redemption, we are able to follow the example of Christ — both within ourselves and in relation to others. We can decide for God and the Kingdom, and not the world. We recognize that we are the temple of God, and thus are not our own (2 Corinthians 6:19, 20). We move forward in our sanctification process (1 Peter 1:13-19) in order to be utterly refashioned in Christ's image (Romans 8:29). Thus, we can proclaim liberty to the captives (Luke 4:18-19). We can love and die for others (John 15:12-13). We can bind the strong man (Matthew 12:28-29). We can call, prepare, and send out disciples (Matthew 28:18-20). We can take up our cross and deny ourselves (16:24-26). We can incarnate our ministries (Hebrews 5:7-10). We can even bring "dead things" to life (Romans 6:12-14).

To equip us for ministry, Christ ushered in the Kingdom of God, his rule on earth. "Repent, for the Kingdom of heaven is at hand" (Matthew 3:2; 12:28; Mark 1:15; Luke 17:21; Colossians 1:13). The Kingdom of God represents righteousness, peace, and joy in the power of the Holy Spirit (Romans 14:17-19). It is a state of blessedness, as man and woman experienced in Eden, in which righteousness overcomes evil and its citizens know only joy and peace. Thus, the righteous Kingdom embodies personal relations characterized by what is just and right, where social relations move toward justice (Matthew 5:20; Hebrews 6:10). It brings moral equity to all (Psalm 119:137; 2 Timothy 4:8). It rights wrongs, showing no favoritism (Nehemiah 9:7-8; Daniel 4:36-37). It also imposes a just law on humans, rewarding obedience and punishing disobedience (Ezekiel 18:5-9; Daniel 9:12, 14; 2 Thessalonians 1:6-7; Revelation 19:1-2).

The peaceful Kingdom embodies personal relations characterized by nonviolence, where social relations move toward peacemaking (Matthew 5:9; John 14:27). It produces tranquility (Acts 9:31), unity (Ephesians 4:1-3; 1 Thessalonians 5:13), and harmony with God (Isaiah 9:6, 7; Romans 5:1; Galatians 5:22-24). The joyful Kingdom embodies personal relations characterized by rejoicing — even if we suffer, where social relations move toward rejoicing — in spite of affliction (Luke 2:10; 1 Corinthians 12:26; 2 Corinthians 7:4; 1 Peter 1:4, 6). It honors faithfulness (Matthew 25:21, 23), celebrates repentance (Luke 15:7, 10, 24), and awaits rejoicing in the hope of future glory (Romans 5:2; 8:18; 12:12).

As a result, we can employ and advance the values of the Kingdom of God to bring healing to the afflicted (Matthew 4:23-24). We are empowered to battle the powers of evil and embody some of the blessings of the future Kingdom in our present age (Matthew 16:18-19). We can seek the Kingdom of God first and God's righteousness (6:31-33). Having received the keys of the Kingdom, we can bind and loose things on earth so they can be bound and loosed in heaven (18:18). In addition, we can make disciples of all nations by baptizing and teaching them (28:18-20). We also can proclaim the gospel to all creation, which is accompanied by signs (Mark 16:15-18).

In addition, we can engage in actions that reflect and advance Christ's rule (Matthew 13:44; Mark 9:43, 45, 47; 10:21; Luke 14:26). We can be aligned at all times with the forthcoming Kingdom (Mark 13:35-36; Luke 12:35-38; 1 Thessalonians 5:2-8; 1 Peter 5:1-10). We can repent and have faith (Matthew 11:20-24; Mark 1:15). We can bring healing to the afflicted (Matthew 4:23-24). Ultimately, this subdues Satan, the "god of this age," and thus delivers people from his enslavement (2 Corinthians 4:4-6). In the process, we take seriously our ambassador role (2 Corinthians 5:20), and thus contribute to Jesus' role as the one and only mediator between God and humanity (1 Timothy 2:5; Hebrews 8:6; 9:15; 12:24).

Not surprisingly, the Kingdom of God is challenged by spiritual and fleshly forces, which seek to infiltrate and negatively alter our thoughts and actions. First, we have to deal with Satan, the "god of this world" (2 Corinthians 4:4-6). Nevertheless, as Jesus entered the strong man's house to defeat Satan and deliver his people from Satan's power (Matthew 12:29), we can proclaim the Kingdom and cast out demons (Luke 10:9, 17). Second, we face false Christs and false prophecies (Matthew 24:4-5). But, as Jesus uncovered the nature and intent of these figures, we can expose and reject these figures and their false teachings (Matthew 24:11, 24; 1 John 2:18; 2 John 7; Revelation 13:1).

Third, we face the apostate, or lukewarm, church, which willfully has rejected Jesus and his teachings (Revelation 3:14-16). Even as it claims non-allegiance due to persecution, temptation, worldliness, defective knowledge of Christ, moral lapse, forsaking worship and spiritual living, and unbelief, we can bring light and speak out against apostasy and empower the body of Christ to identify it and disassociate itself from it (Matthew 24:9; Luke 8:13; 2 Timothy 4:4; Hebrews 3:12; 6:4-6; 10:25-31; 1 John 2:19). Finally, we face our own flesh, our sinful nature (see Romans 8:4-12; 1 Corinthians 15:50-53). As Jesus revealed that the Spirit gives life even though the flesh is weak, limited, and worldly, we can seek the fruit of the Spirit and reject the flesh (see John 3:6; 6:63; 8:15; Galatians 5:17-21; 1 Peter 2:11; 1 John 2:16).

Christ's Body Can Employ Holistic Ministry

These challenges should remind you that the world is still in captivity:

> The creation itself also will be delivered from the bondage of corruption into the glorious liberty of the children of God. For we know that the whole creation groans and labors with birth pangs together until now. (Romans 8:21-22)

In fact, it is God's children who are free. You are in this world, even as you are not of this world. In the midst of captivity, Christ has empowered his body, the church, to carry out its mission: "I will give you the keys of the kingdom of heaven, and whatever you bind on earth shall be bound in heaven, and whatever you loose on earth shall be loosed in heaven" (Matthew 16:18-19).

Put another way, Christ has called you to adopt and apply *holistic ministry*, a prophetic act of word and deed, a Christ-centered approach to life in which you live, serve, and lead in a godly way (Romans 15:17-19; 1 Peter 2:4-5). In the process of practicing holistic ministry, you become an instrument that releases God's power of liberation and life. You engage and confront your community and the powers to help bring about personal and social transformation. Thus, you produce spiritual and moral change among people, the church, and society.

Toward this end, you increase your understanding of your lot in life

(Romans 12:1-2). You live out your days in a way that impacts you and the people and institutions that interact with you, both directly and indirectly (12:3-8). You also become holistic, and work to improve the social fabric of society (12:9-21). Ultimately, your faith becomes public, as you address policy issues in your community. As you grow as a Christian, and as someone who practices holistic ministry, you will strengthen what I call the Four Pillars of Community Life: *families, schools, community-based organizations,* and *churches.*[3]

Holistic Ministry Is Humane and Restorative

As you await his return, Christ's people proclaim his good news to all creation (Acts 1:8): in Jerusalem — their immediate community; in Judea — their surrounding community; in Samaria — those whom they would not deem deserving of redemption and reconciliation; and to the end of the earth — faraway places that have not heard the gospel message. For this reason, Christ gifted you with the power and guidance of the Holy Spirit. Thus, you proclaim and carry out his Spirit-filled message to bring about God's peace (John 14:25-27).

Central to holistic ministry is that you engage in personal growth and community revitalization (Acts 2:42-47; 6:1-6). You connect their values and beliefs to your commitment to your families and communities. Thus, you serve the larger community, and prepare to lead community efforts. At times, you create new institutions and collaborations that meet the present or future needs of the communities. In the process, you also draw on the collective gifts in the church and develop a mature understanding of the gospel (Ephesians 4:13). This way, you avoid employing worldly or fleshly values and social constructions that get in the way of the peace, joy, and righteousness of the Kingdom of God.

The Four Principles of Holistic Ministry Guide Us

As a holistic person, you are driven by the Four Principles of Holistic Ministry: *liberation, healing, community,* and *transformation,* which represent your

---

3. There may be other pillars (for instance, businesses and government), but these four institutions are the ones in which the largest numbers of community members are a part.

walk in Christ (Galatians 4:3, 6-7; Hebrews 6:1-2). These principles facilitate spiritual and moral change, which in turn leads to socio-political and economic change. Through liberation, you are freed personally from the social conditioning and systems that do not serve the people and institutions they were created to help (John 8:31-36). No longer are you captive to social, religious, national, and ethnic norms and conditions that drive you away from Christ's message (Galatians 1:10). You also are freed structurally from the world's systems and structures, or their socializing agencies (Luke 20:25). Even as you are subject to the governing authorities (Romans 13:1; 1 Peter 2:13-14), you still obey God rather than man, even if it puts your personal safety at risk (Acts 5:29-32). Liberation propels you to follow Christ's lead and serve those in captivity (Luke 4:18), who are most in need of spiritual and physical freedom.

Through healing, you become a wounded healer (Isaiah 53:5-6), not in a condescending way of feeling superior to wounded people. You experience divine grace, which produces humility in dealing with others. Thus, you comfort others in a godly manner (2 Corinthians 1:3-4). You acknowledge that you too were captive, and Christ also died for your sins (1 Peter 2:24-25). So when you encounter people who gratify the desires of their flesh, you recall having satisfied your own fleshly desires. For this reason, you draw on the fruit of the Spirit (Galatians 5:22), and refrain from becoming conceited, and from provoking and envying others (5:26). You restore others gently, keeping an eye to avoid being tempted (6:1). In addition, you accept suffering as a result of being one with Christ (Philippians 1:29). You accept that it connects you to Christ, and to those who have experienced suffering.

Through community, you become one community *(koinonia)* and serve the larger community *(diakonia)*. You congregate with other wounded healers and establish authentic communities — churches — in the midst of a captive society (Hebrews 10:24-25). Together, you help bring about Christ's peace and justice in word and deed (Acts 2:42-47). You advance Christ's message of liberation to the larger society (Acts 1:8). Thus, you go to your immediate community (Jerusalem), surrounding community (Judea), adversaries and objectors of the gospel (Samaria), and those who have not heard the gospel (the end of the earth). In the process, you draw on your solid community foundation to engage and confront others effectively within the captive society (Galatians 5:13-15). All of this happens with the guidance and direction of the Holy Spirit, who endows you with gifts to use for the common good (1 Corinthians 12:7).

Finally, through transformation, you become a catalyst for ongoing renewal in your personal life and the community at large, thus resulting in perpetual growth (Romans 12:1-2). This transformation is both personal and social, which represents your ongoing change to the image of Christ (2 Corinthians 3:18). It suggests escalating levels of glory, which culminates in the final glory with Christ's return and the full consummation of the Kingdom of God (Philippians 3:20-21). You experience glory in your lifetime, provided you reflect the obedient Christ and not the disobedient Adam (1 Corinthians 15:21-22, 45).

Through personal transformation, you are faithful to the Rule of God (Colossians 2:6-7). You receive the whole counsel of God (Acts 20:27). You follow the blueprint for Christian living (Matthew 5–7). You set your mind on things that are above (Colossians 3:2-17). You hold fast to what is good (Romans 12:9–13:7). You walk by the Spirit (Galatians 5:16-26). You teach sound doctrine (Titus 2:1-8). Thus, you become a fisher of other men and women. You use the power God gave you to bind the strongman (Matthew 12:29). You also act on Christ's commission to serve and lead God's creation (28:18-20; Mark 16:15-18). Interestingly, Christ commissioned both those who worshiped and those who doubted him (Matthew 28:18). Either way, Christ commissioned you!

Through social transformation, you stand up for peace and justice (2 Timothy 2:22-26), which occurs when you take responsibility for others. Toward this end, you turn to the example of Christ's public ministry, which presents a blueprint for Christian service (Luke 4:18-19). You also help build an authentic Christian community (Acts 2:42-47; 6:1-6). You strive for community development (Nehemiah 1–8). You also resort to systemic engagement when the treatment of people and communities violates Kingdom of God values (Esther 2–10).

Holistic Ministry Calls for Living, Serving, and Leading in a Godly Way

Along with the holistic principles, you receive guidance and direction from the Holy Spirit and the Scriptures to live, serve, and lead in a godly way (Ecclesiastes 12:11-14; Romans 6:20-23). Holistic living, service, and leadership reflect the three significant areas in which you practice holistic ministry. Through Holistic Living, you love God by strengthening your spiritual (heart), emotional (soul), mental (mind), and physical (strength) dimensions (Matthew 22:37). You love others (or neighbors) by strengthening your social dimension, and you love yourself by developing your self-knowledge, identity, worth, determination, reliance, and defense (Matthew 22:39). You also deny yourself by meeting the needs of others and committing to suffer for their sake (Luke 9:23).

Through Holistic Service, you engage and confront both your community (Esther 2:5-7, 10-11; 4:5-17; Nehemiah 2:17-18; 5:6-8) and the powers (Esther 4:1-3; 8:8, 10; Nehemiah 2:1-8; 4:7-17). To engage your community, you establish relationships with people within the Christian community and serve as instruments of transformation within the church and parachurch institutions. To confront your community, you call your community to submit to God's will, practice what it professes, and reject unfair doctrines or practices. To engage the powers, you establish relationships with people outside of the Christian community and serve as instruments of transformation within the system and society. Finally, to confront the powers, you call the institutional systems and structures to submit to God's plan and his Kingdom and renounce unjust decrees or norms.

Through Holistic Leadership, you prepare (2 Timothy 1:13-14) by receiving formal instruction, participating in hands-on exercises, and accepting the call to perform in leadership and/or advisory roles. You perform as a holistic servant leader (2:1-2) by carrying out leadership and/or advisory roles within your families, schools, churches, and community institutions. You also produce other holistic servant leaders (4:1-5) by reaching out to others who exhibit holistic servant leadership qualities and preparing these emerging leaders to lead people and institutions.

CHAPTER 3

You Also Are Called to Minister in Captivity!

$\mathcal{M}$

S o there you have it! Can you see that our society indeed is captive? I
hope you can. I also hope you recognize that even in the midst of
captivity God continues to bring forth his plan to liberate his creation.
To think that the almighty God has chosen to educate, equip, and empower his people to be part of his perfect plan for redemption and restoration! Our voices can actually reach many more people than our immediate reality! Our actions actually can impact much more than our
immediate surroundings! I praise and thank you, Lord, for this gift and
opportunity!

Now, you may be thinking, *I get that we are in a captive world and that
Christ will complete his restoration work in the End Times. I can even buy that God
involved special people, like the prophets, and even our present-day pastors, elders,
and deacons. But I still don't see how God wants me to do anything more than be a
good person and a good citizen.* Well, if you think this way, you are not alone!
Many Christians have adopted the idea that goodness is an individual
pursuit. As long as I do good works, it is fine that I focus primarily on my
immediate family and friends. The apostle James, however, provides a
different view.

"Faith by itself, if it does not have works, is dead" (James 2:17). I am
sure you have heard this familiar verse before; you may even have said it
yourself. In fact, you may feel this verse vindicates you, that indeed your
works for your family and friends should suffice. But James does not focus exclusively on family and friends in his explanation of what he
means when he says this (2:15). In fact, the brother or sister he mentions

is a brother or sister in Christ, very possibly a brother or sister of another family, whom you may not have met formally.

In fact, James gives even greater clarity as to the type of brother or sister about whom he was concerned, and about whom he expects us to be concerned.

> If a brother or sister is naked and destitute of daily food, and one of you says to them, "Depart in peace, be warmed and filled," but you do not give them the things which are needed for the body, what does it profit? (2:15-16)

James undoubtedly was concerned about the poor and needy among us — the brother or sister who did not have the means to fend for himself or herself. Of course, it is valid to help one's clan. In fact, this is expected. But Jesus himself was not satisfied with this narrow perspective:

> For if you love those who love you, what reward do you have? Do not even the tax collectors do the same? And if you greet your brethren only, what do you do more than others? Do not even the tax collectors do so? (Matthew 5:46-48)

James is introducing in this passage an expectation for the common good that goes beyond what you do for loved ones in your immediate surroundings.

Indeed, James is summoning us to be concerned about the whole world around us, particularly those in need. Earlier in chapter 2, James warns us against the bias even we Christians have against those in our society with the least means:

> But you have dishonored the poor man. Do not the rich oppress you and drag you into the courts? Do they not blaspheme that noble name by which you are called? (James 2:6-7)

Not just the rich, but also the systems and structures we participate in oppress the poor and needy. And it is not just worldly people and citizens. Regrettably, Christians and the church as an institution have perpetrated this treatment toward the least in our society. So how do we remedy this individualistic and indifferent attitude exercised by too many in the body of Christ? By accepting the call to minister in captivity!

God Has Called You to Minister in Captivity

So what, then, is a call? A call is when God ("the caller") makes a claim on the life or time of a person and/or an organization ("the called one"). The caller charges the called one to present an appeal or demand to a target audience (of people, groups, organizations, etc.). In turn, the called one charges the target audience to adopt a way of living that will yield concrete change for the target audience and for the society at large, sometimes to address present circumstances and sometimes to make recompense for past actions or inactions. Yet while the caller gives the called one great responsibility, he does not hold the called one responsible for the ultimate response of the target audience.

When a person is called to minister or serve in captivity, God summons the called one to help bring about the *personal and social transformation* of a target audience or the society at large. The called one recognizes that God is the originator of the message: "I will be with your mouth and teach you what you shall say" (Exodus 4:12). "Do not say, 'I am a youth'; for you shall go to all to whom I send you, and whatever I command you, you shall speak" (Jeremiah 1:7). In turn, the called one points the target audience to God's plan and purpose, inspiring its members to trust and rely on God. Ultimately, the called one accepts the call to minister, and no longer considers his or her personal views as vital to the administration of the call: "He must increase, but I must decrease" (John 3:30). Thus, God's purpose and plan prevails in word and deed.

Components of a God-Given Call

Very early in my ministry, I understood that there were particular components of a God-given call to minister in captivity. Through the example of the prophet Ezekiel, I derived six general components of a God-given call: (1) *transcendent vision,* (2) *historical context,* (3) *prophetic integrity,* (4) *incarnation,* (5) *paradox,* and (6) *God's gifts.* Of course, Ezekiel was called to minister in the particular situation of Judah's captivity in Babylon. Like all calls, his was not a generic call. Still, these components have applied in various situations of captivity in my ministry, whether in Sunset Park, the Lower East Side, or the Southwest Bronx. And they will apply in your ministry as well!

Transcendent Vision

> Now it came to pass in the thirtieth year, in the fourth month, on the fifth day of the month, as I was among the captives by the River Chebar, that the heavens were opened and I saw visions of God. (Ezekiel 1:1)

A transcendent vision is one that goes beyond space and time, and reveals the glory and power of God's Kingdom. While the full realization of the Kingdom of God lies in the future, at times it can invade human history, and you taste the powers of the coming age in our present reality. A transcendent vision helps you rise above your culture, tradition, and religiosity. It challenges you to deny the essence of who you think you are. It helps you embrace change and rise above your circumstances, and transcend your environment and social conditioning. It connects you more to people and to your community, as you do not have your head in the clouds.

A transcendent vision also points to a better future. When God gives you one, you have a clear sense of the end result. You also have a clear sense of your destination, which keeps you from falling into busy work. You have a greater criteria and frame of reference by which you can judge everything that happens to you daily. Thus, you can have hope in the midst of captivity. This is the case even as girls get pregnant at thirteen and fourteen, and young people are joining gangs — even in the suburbs. It also keeps you from the captivity of affluence, be it in the inner city or in the suburbs. It humbles you before the presence of God (Ezekiel 1:28). It reveals God's holiness, grace, and calling (Isaiah 6:1-8). What's more, it reveals God's new city, the New Jerusalem (Revelation 21:10-11; 21:22-27). Thus, you accept that being a lawyer, banker, or real estate magnate alone does not make you free.

Historical Context

Look again at Ezekiel 1:1. Notice how the transcendent vision comes in the midst of a specific historical context. The vision is concrete, not abstract; it invades the prevailing historical context. Too many people in our world have visions that have no relevancy to where they live or to the times. Their view of the Kingdom of God is so future-oriented that it does not speak to any present-day reality like their community's state of affairs.

Historical context connects your vision to the people around you. It connects you to the people who are in the situation of captivity God has called you to address, and it works through people's choices and consequences. As the God of Abraham, Isaac, and Jacob, God intertwined his plan with our human story. God dealt with Abraham and the choices he made. Abraham took Hagar for his wife, which resulted in Ishmael's birth before Isaac. Jacob became Israel after a sometimes chaotic life with his parents, brother, wives, and children. Their stories were not identical, but God dealt with them in the midst of the world they lived and created for themselves. In the same way God will connect with you in the particularities of your real-life situation.

Prophetic Integrity

> For they are impudent and stubborn children. I am sending you to them, and you shall say to them, "Thus says the Lord God." As for them, whether they hear or whether they refuse — for they are a rebellious house — yet they will know that a prophet has been among them. (Ezekiel 2:4-5)

Those who minister in captivity speak for God, or from the perspective of God, to the society of their day. You may not compromise this, even if you are confronted and surrounded by principalities and powers, both personal and structural. You become God's instrument to measure whether the society is meeting his standards of peace and justice for his creation.

To be a prophet is not simply to be some kind of seer, who only predicts the future. Rather, you speak to how society's conduct affects people in the present, especially the most vulnerable — the poor, the marginalized, the widow, the orphan, the stranger, and so on. You address the total needs of people and society — the totality of life. Like Jesus, you bridge the spiritual and the secular. In addition, with the grace and power of the Triune God, you help empower the church with all of its gifts and diversity of ministries so that it can be a sign of God's Kingdom and thus improve our society.

Incarnation

> Then I came to the captives at Tel Abib, who dwelt by the River
> Chebar; and I sat where they sat, and remained there astonished
> among them seven days. (Ezekiel 3:15)

As God incarnated himself in the Son, and the Son in the church — his
body — so must your ministry incarnate itself in the community. The
end goal in Christianity is not *nirvana,* or detachment from the world, but
the full realization of the Kingdom of God. Christ chose to incarnate,
and not to detach. He sought to serve in the midst of the captivity, and
thus brought restoration. "As you sent me into the world, so I have sent
them into the world" (John 17:18).

Incarnation is not about staying on the mountaintop, or about dis-
missing the sinful oppression in which people live. It is about engaging it,
incarnating oneself in the midst of it. It is to realize captivity's horrific effects on the human experience and then to *do* something about it. In fact,
the increase in compassion has a direct relationship on our level of incarnation. For example, by being incarnational in the life of Esther (who was
inside the gate), Mordecai (who was outside the gate) showed her love
and care, which influenced her to serve her community (Esther 2:10-11;
4:5-8; 13:14). This also was the case for Jesus, whose love and care guided
Peter to commit to serve others (John 21:15-18).

Paradox[1]

> So the Spirit lifted me up and took me away, and I went in bitterness,
> in the heat of my spirit; but the hand of the Lord was strong upon
> me. (Ezekiel 3:14)

---

1. I developed an appreciation of the idea of paradox through the life of Rev. Dr. Justo L.
González, who interacted with the dominant culture from the perspective of a Hispanic in
the mainline church. I also was impacted by his theological critique of the dominant culture, which was particularly helpful to me while I was an executive in the Reformed
Church in America in the 1970s. In the past two decades I have been influenced by the following works in particular: *Mañana: Christian Theology from a Hispanic Perspective* (Nashville:
Abingdon Press, 1990); *Santa Biblia: The Bible through Hispanic Eyes* (Nashville: Abingdon
Press, 1996); and *The Liberating Pulpit* (Eugene, OR: Wipf & Stock Publishers, 2002; co-
written with Catherine González).

Ezekiel felt bitter and angry at what his people were experiencing; he recognized his own sense of unworthiness as he experienced God's voice. But he did not stop his ministry in the midst of captivity. After all, the Holy Spirit was present and in control. You might feel overwhelmed when you see and experience the effects of the Fall and of captivity in your personal, family, and community lives every day. You might even internalize the notion that things cannot change; a sense of impotence could grab hold of you. At the same time, you also might experience an opposite emotion: hope! You recognize that you have been called by God and experience his grace. Thus, like Jesus, who cried over the coming destruction of Jerusalem (Matthew 24:1-2), you cry over the people and the cities. Also, like Moses, who broke the tablets after coming down Mount Sinai and seeing God's people worshiping false idols (Exodus 32:19), you will break some tablets in Jesus' name.

God's Gifts: The Holy Spirit and the Bible [2]

> And he said to me, "Son of man, stand on your feet, and I will speak to you." Then the Spirit entered me when he spoke to me, and set me on my feet; and I heard him who spoke to me. (Ezekiel 2:1-2)

Indeed, your ministry in captivity cannot be based on the power of your own intellect or eloquence, your human intuition, or the power of any institution that you belong to. Ultimately, what makes you stand is God's gift of the Holy Spirit. He authorizes, or sets you apart, for a particular service (Isaiah 61:1; Luke 4:18). Jesus himself was anointed with the Holy Spirit for service (John 1:32-33; Acts 4:27; 10:38; 2 Corinthians 1:21-22). So was Peter, who after being filled with the Holy Spirit at Pentecost delivered an anointed message that led to three thousand souls being saved in one day (Acts 2:4-41).

---

2. Here, I was influenced by Rev. Dr. Eldin Villafañe's insight that the call of the Holy Spirit in our lives is not limited to the personal, but also has social-political-economic-cultural implications. His impact on me was very personal and experiential because he was an indigenous Pentecostal theologian who remained in his immediate religious community, the Assemblies of God. He tried to provide leadership to that community, while also serving the entire body of Christ. In the last two decades, I have been impacted by his later writings: *The Liberating Spirit: Toward an Hispanic American Pentecostal Social Ethic* (Grand Rapids: Eerdmans, 1993); and *Seek the Peace of the City: Reflections on Urban Ministries* (Grand Rapids: Eerdmans, 1995).

Ezekiel also addressed the significance of the Holy Scriptures:

> "But you, son of man, hear what I say to you. Do not be rebellious
> like that rebellious house; open your mouth and eat what I give you."
> Now when I looked, there was a hand stretched out to me; and be-
> hold, a scroll of a book was in it. Then he spread it before me; and
> there was writing on the inside and on the outside, and written on it
> were lamentations and mourning and woe. Moreover he said to me,
> "Son of man, eat what you find; eat this scroll, and go, speak to the
> house of Israel." So I opened my mouth, and he caused me to eat that
> scroll. (2:8-3:2)

Your ministry in captivity cannot be based on mere scientific and tech-
nological methodology, even if these tools are able to help you. To be effective, you must be centered on God's eternal gift of the Word of God.
Jesus makes clear that keeping God's Word is essential to loving him, and
to being loved by the Father — the author of the Word (John 14:23-24;
2 Peter 1:20-21). In fact, the biblical truths and lessons of the Old and New
Testaments enable you to make effective life decisions (see Jeremiah 36:2;
Zephaniah 2:3; Romans 15:4; 2 Timothy 3:16-17).

Purpose and Scope of Your God-Given Call

As you absorb the components of a God-given call, keep in mind that
God is calling you to minister in captivity for his glory.

> Therefore we also pray always for you that our God would count you
> worthy of this calling, and fulfill all the good pleasure of his good-
> ness and the work of faith with power, that the name of our Lord Je-
> sus Christ may be glorified in you, and you in him, according to the
> grace of our God and the Lord Jesus Christ. (2 Thessalonians 1:11-12)

Not surprisingly, God does not prescribe a universal call to ministry.
One size does not fit all! The God of Abraham, Isaac, and Jacob dealt
with each of his servants in the specific context of captivity they lived
in and created for themselves. It was there that God opened the door
for their redemption and restoration, and allowed them to become involved in the redemption and restoration of those around them. In the

same light, it is in today's society that God has called you to minister in captivity!

Of course, you may be thinking now about the call of men and women in the Bible and of Christ himself — even of your pastor and other church leaders. Compared to them, you may reason that God could not possibly call you to anything significant. Again, you might think that as long as you maintain a good home, keep a job, and obey the laws, you will have done your part in the midst of God's creation. If you do not add to the captivity around you, you will have met God's call for a godly life.

While this may seem to comply sufficiently with your understanding of God's call for you, Jesus reveals that God's call includes more than a personal victory. In fact, your individual call is entirely connected to Jesus' call to service.

> But whoever desires to become great among you, let him be your servant. And whoever desires to be first among you, let him be your slave — just as the Son of Man did not come to be served, but to serve, and to give his life a ransom for many. (Matthew 20:26-28)

Paul champions Jesus as the model for servanthood; for him, the ultimate servanthood can be seen in Jesus' obedience to the point of humiliation and death.

> Let this mind be in you which was also in Christ Jesus, who, being in the form of God, did not consider it robbery to be equal with God, but made himself of no reputation, taking the form of a bondservant, and coming in the likeness of men. And being found in appearance as a man, he humbled himself and became obedient to the point of death, even the death of the cross. (Philippians 2:5-8)

Indeed, Paul saw our call as an extension of our service to Jesus:

> Be kindly affectionate to one another with brotherly love, in honor giving preference to one another; not lagging in diligence, fervent in spirit, serving the Lord; rejoicing in hope, patient in tribulation, continuing steadfastly in prayer; distributing to the needs of the saints, given to hospitality. (Romans 12:10-13)

Given what some of Jesus' disciples and the members of the early church did, you may think that God's call involves monumental tasks or heroic endeavors. However, the truth is that God seeks mainly ordinary men and women, whom he raises for primarily ordinary tasks that bring about his glory. "Therefore, brethren, seek out from among you seven men of good reputation, full of the Holy Spirit and wisdom, whom we may appoint over this business" (Acts 6:3). These men were not asked to replace the apostles, who were responsible for praying and preaching the Word of God. They simply were chosen to ensure that the Greek Christian widows received resources from the church's daily distribution. As a result, the apostles could perform their duties, which increased the number of disciples (6:7).

So what qualified these seven men for their duty? They had good reputations and were full of the Spirit and godly wisdom. In fact, throughout the Scriptures, these were the distinctive characteristics of the people God called. And not many of them are famous. In fact, can you name all seven deacons, all twelve apostles, the twelve so-called Minor Prophets, or Israel's judges? Probably not, but each of these men and women was given both a general and a special call, which they faithfully carried out.

Even those who were considered weak possessed spiritual gifts that helped them carry out their ministry. In his infinite wisdom, God made the weak vital to the entire body, granting them the greatest honor (1 Corinthians 12:22-23). Thus, those with more obvious gifting could not separate themselves from the "less honorable" among them. In turn, the body was to be united and its members were to care for one another (12:25). This allowed for the greatest number of disciples to be involved in carrying out Jesus' Great Commission and to meet the mandate of the body of Christ.

For all these reasons, you should accept your God-given call! Truly, I believe that, if you persevere, you will live every day to its fullest and without regrets. You will live life in abundance and gladly give more than you receive. You will discover and use the God-given gifts and talents that are within you. You will learn and adopt a language that will facilitate others following you. You will do something to respond to the things about which you complain. You also will be free of vices and other fleshly desires.

At the same time, I do not want to downplay the challenges of accepting the call. I have had my share of personal, professional, and ministry trials and heartache, and so will you. At times, I have moved forward only because of the knowledge that God is with me — having few or no financial, human, or physical resources. This was not always comforting to everyone around me; there were some people who advised me to take a more conservative approach — the safer route. Many things the Lord has called me to do may not have appeared safe or sound to others. Yet God has always delivered and kept me, and I trust that he will continue to keep me safe as I maintain my ministry in the midst of captivity.

Again, I will not lie to you. You will face challenges as you minister in captivity! Some of them will be external, and others internal. Like Jonah who was sent to minister to the enemies of his own people, you may have to carry out tasks that do not seem to make sense or to be aligned with God's purpose. You may even have to face dangerous situations or your own past, which may have been or may be out of alignment with God's will. You may need to use your gifts or talents, but you may have wasted them or failed to develop or strengthen them in the past. You also may simply be paralyzed by fear, having convinced yourself that you are not equipped to carry out your call.

At different levels, I have had to face these and other challenges. But after over forty-five years, I have learned to embrace Paul's assessment of his Christian life as my own:

> Therefore most gladly I will rather boast in my infirmities, that the power of Christ may rest upon me. Therefore I take pleasure in infirmities, in reproaches, in needs, in persecutions, in distresses, for Christ's sake. For when I am weak, then I am strong. (2 Corinthians 12:9-10)

I also have trusted that by sharing in Christ's suffering, I will "rejoice to the extent that [I] partake of Christ's sufferings, that when his glory is revealed, [I] may also be glad with exceeding joy" (1 Peter 4:13). If you think about Jonah's ministry again, you should recognize that not all challenges or storms that enter your life are demonic. In fact, God allows some storms in order to bring you back to his will. Still, he provides resources in the midst of these storms, even when you have resisted your call. You actually may need to rid yourself of things that are out of alignment with God's will. If this is the case, you may have to deal with the storms until you remove them from your life. In fact, only when you throw your obstacles "overboard" will you be in a position to get back into the will of God and succeed in your call to minister in captivity (Jonah 1).

Draw from My Call to Minister in Captivity

Looking back at my more than forty-five years of ministry, I see that I learned various lessons in accepting God's call to minister in various situations of captivity, which I now pass on to you in this book's remaining chapters. Overall, I feel joy knowing I proclaimed the gospel of Jesus Christ. Many came to Christ through me, and became mature and thriving church and community leaders. Many adopted the practice of holistic ministry and contributed to the development of their communities. Even my children, both biological and spiritual, have followed me in service to the church and the community. In the process, many have increased their service and hospitality; increased their self-awareness and collective awareness and responsibility; enhanced their interpersonal relationships; and provided greater care for the poor and marginalized. In addition, their quality of life and their communities have improved. Even the course of history changed for some of them. I can honestly say that my labor has not been in vain! Who would have thought this, given how I started my journey to act on God's call to minister in captivity?

Assume Responsibility for Your Social Reality

I remember the start of my call like it was yesterday! It was the summer of 1961, and I was fifteen years old and living with my parents in Spanish Harlem. I had a respectful and loving relationship with my parents. I also had many friends and felt part of my neighborhood culture. But I struggled in school, and because I stuttered I felt socially awkward at times; some of my friends sometimes made fun of me. In the midst of this reality, my father announced that he was moving the family to Brooklyn, New York, because his factory was relocating there.

We wound up in the middle of an Italian neighborhood in what today is Ocean Hill/Brownsville, living in a two-family house owned by an elderly Italian man. I suddenly found myself in a neighborhood whose residents I had, from my family's time in Spanish Harlem, previously seen as my enemy. Yet I had no other place to go, so I had to relate to these people. I was shocked when the neighborhood Italian youth embraced me. Even though they called me Pancho, I learned to cope.

That September, I went to junior high school in the neighborhood of what is today Bedford-Stuyvesant. Through one of my new school friends, I connected to a group of Puerto Ricans that lived about five blocks from where I lived. They were older, out of school, working, and already had girlfriends. After that, I gradually disconnected from people in my neighborhood, and my life seemed oddly familiar again. Even though I was in a different borough, I was connecting to the same lifestyle. For some reason, basketball also followed me and I quickly became captain of the junior high school team.

Not too long after, I stopped going to school and started hanging out with my new friends. I knew intuitively that the right thing to do was to go to school and embrace my opportunity for a scholarship. But I still found myself drawn to the lifestyle of my friends and my environment. While the coach at Franklin K. Lane High School talked to me about a college scholarship, I just did not see it as a real option for me. I even made the high school varsity basketball team, quickly getting significant playtime my first year at the school. But I still ended up with my friends at the bleachers by the athletic fields — even though I often got a strange feeling that I really did not belong with them.

Even at that age, I wondered why so much conflict existed between people. We felt hate, animosity, as a group toward Italians. But individually, many of the neighborhood Italians and Puerto Ricans got along. I don't want to get *West Side Story* on you, but I began to wonder how people groups could collectively have broken relationships, while, individually, they could rise above their group identity! Even then, I intuitively understood that this rising-above represented the way things ought to be. Yet like Nehemiah, I had to confess that my family and I contributed to this problem (Nehemiah 1:6). And, like Isaiah, I had to declare that my community added to it as well (Isaiah 6:4-5).

Recognize God's Call When He Engages or Confronts You

Later that summer, my life took a radical turn after I went through an experience that I have come to understand as God's call on my life. One late afternoon, I was walking down Fulton Street in Ocean Hill/Brownsville and I heard music coming out of the Fulton Terrace Hall. I thought it was a dance, so I peeked inside. To my surprise, it was some type of religious service. At the door were attractive young ladies with long hair, no make-up, and conservative dresses. They invited me inside. I said no, but agreed to return soon.

Immediately, I went to my block and told my friends. Four of them came back with me. The music was upbeat. Organ. Tambourines. People were shouting, "Hallelujah!" and "Praise the Lord!" It brought me back to the mid-1950s when I went with my mother and aunt to the Spanish Bethel Pentecostal Church in Spanish Harlem. We enjoyed the singing, preaching, and personal testimonies. Reverends Sam and Efrain Felix were the preachers. They spoke our language, having had personal experience with the gang and drug culture. Yet we still made fun of everything, talked to each other, and yelled out and made comments. We also went in and out of the room, and sometimes went outside to smoke.

After the service, we agreed to go back and attend the revival services every day, even though we didn't take them seriously. One night, the service focused on healing and the evangelist asked for people who needed healing to go up to the altar. One of my friends went up faking a limp in his leg, and the evangelists anointed him with oil and prayed for him. Then he said he was healed, and the people exploded in praises and prayers of gratitude. The evangelists had him parade up and down the platform, showing that he was healed. At the same time, he was winking at us, and we were slapping each other high fives and making fun of everything that had happened. We went home laughing about the experience, but still agreed to return.

The last night of the revival, the evangelists prayed for us and encouraged us to continue going to church. They connected us to Centro Evangélico y Misionero (Gospel and Missionary Center) on Osborne Street in Brownsville. It was a small storefront Pentecostal church. When we got there, we saw over twenty young ladies sitting together. There were also young men, including evangelist Hector Seda, all dressed in suits and ties while we were in our street clothes. Some people were experiencing manifestations of the Holy Spirit. Our presence seemed to intimidate the traditional adult members, who I thought were giving us dirty looks. But it did not stop us from returning.

One night, the church held a special evangelistic service, with a guest speaker known for possessing the spiritual gift of healing. Toward the end of the service, he made an altar call for those who wanted to be filled with the Holy Spirit. Again, the same friend who had faked a limp responded to the call and we followed him up. The preacher asked us to get on our knees and begin repeating with him utterances of praise to God. I remember looking around, surrounded by people on their knees who were uttering these phrases. My eyes locked directly on my friend, who began to shake uncontrollably, then fell on his back and rolled around on the floor. I was startled and became confused. Was it possible that he had received the Spirit as the preacher had said?

My friend started shaking and rolling violently. His eyes were closed and he started screeching and screaming, as if in pain. He also began throwing the chairs near him, like he had superhuman strength. The preacher and the other leaders expressed concern, as they could not control this physical outburst. At this point, the pastor declared that my friend was filled with an evil spirit. I was confused and angry, because I did not understand what was happening. It felt otherworldly to me, not real. It was like we were in an *Exorcist* movie.

I tried talking to my friend, but he was unresponsive. He did not even recognize us. His voice changed and he started attacking my friend and me, saying that the "people" in him were going to kill us and that we would die that night. We, of course, tried to present a macho attitude, but in reality we were scared. We had never seen these types of manifestations. It was a very scary feeling. He kept saying again and again, "I'm going to kill y'all tonight. This is your last day on earth." This ordeal lasted at least an hour, continuing even after the service before finally subsiding. The church leaders stayed behind and prayed with us until he regained consciousness.

We left the church that night in great fear. We walked home through very hostile projects, where people constantly were being killed. Along the way, the voice I heard coming from my friend's mouth was resonating in my mind. *We're going to kill you. Tonight is your last night.* I asked my friend if he knew what had happened, but he did not remember anything. He just felt pain in his body. So I shared with him what the pastor had said — that he was possessed by an evil spirit and that God had a plan and purpose for him and the rest of us. As I spoke, I became anxious and fearful. We talked about what we had just gone through, and how they had said that we were being attacked by the devil. In spite of it all, we agreed to return to the church.

Fortunately, we reached home safely, and we were greatly relieved. The next day, we heard through the grapevine that, at about the same time we usually passed through those projects, some young people had been killed. Of course, we had not passed at the usual time because we had been held up in church. This was very traumatic for us, and we thought about not going back to the church because these incidents were clearly beyond our control. We suddenly found ourselves in a supernatural world of which we had little knowledge. We knew there was a power there. We also knew it included evil, and that evil was determined to destroy us. Yet this time, we resisted the spiritual powers, and were able to triumph over the urge to submit to the evil and demonic powers.

On another night, a young woman at the church was lifted in the spirit of prophecy and brought a message to the pastor saying that this time had all been a trial for the church, and that the church would experience a great blessing and growth. As she was speaking to the congregation in the sanctuary, my friend was receiving healing and the baptism of the Holy Spirit. He was brought from the prayer room to the sanctuary, and testified that he had been delivered from the evil spirits.

As you can see, my encounter with God was dramatic like that of Paul (Acts 9:3-19), whom Jesus confronted on the road to Damascus. I had gained new sight (9:18). I was interpreting to my friends what happened to us. I was convincing them to return to the church, even though I was not sure what would happen next. I disconnected from negative influences. I enrolled at a three-year Bible Institute, even though I did not like high school. I was even stuttering less. I also became a youth leader in the church, and I started preparing for my eventual vocation — pastoral ministry.

Of course, not all calls are dramatic like mine. Many calls are gradual, like that of Peter, with whom Jesus interacted over the course of three years. Either way, the call brings light, even if it does not immediately bring clarity. Paul had to wait to hear his call through another disciple. Also, Peter, who learned directly from Jesus all those years, would not understand his call until Pentecost (Acts 2–3), and really not until he visited Cornelius after the insistence of the Lord (Acts 10).

Accept Your Call as the Entry Point to Your New Journey

My initial call to ministry was a defining moment in my spiritual journey. Here I was a jobless, stuttering high-school dropout, who would spend every waking day hanging out with mostly older friends. Not exactly what the world would consider the raw material for success! But on that fateful day, when I was on my knees and repeated the utterances of praise to God that the guest speaker asked my friends and me to repeat, I knew my life had changed. Like Jesus (Matthew 3:16) and Paul (Acts 9:17), I had been baptized with the Holy Spirit! At the same time, something told me that I had not fully realized the total extent of my call. This would become clearer over the next forty-five years.

After Fulton Terrace Hall, my belief systems changed. Christ and the church became my network of friends and family. I attended church and read the Bible almost daily, and prayed daily. Lamentably, my old friends did not accept my change, so we drifted apart. Like the apostle Paul, I had turned my back on my previous alliances and experiences. Initially I had conflict with my father, who had not been serving the Lord in his life. But he ultimately accepted Jesus as his Lord and Savior, which naturally transformed our relationship, as well as those with his friends and family.

Less than a year later, I was enrolled in the denomination's Bible Institute at our church, and had started preparing formally for my ministry call. Three years later, I had graduated and was asked by the institute director to teach at the institute. During that same time, I served as the president of my church's youth organization. My pastor, Rev. José Falero, who had become the district presbyter, also recommended me to be the exhorter within the denomination, which was the first level toward ordination. I even began preaching at other churches across New York State.

A year later, after I turned twenty, my pastor asked me to become the pastor of El Camino Pentecostal Church, a small storefront church in Sunset Park, Brooklyn. I understood this as the culmination of my preparation, as well as an affirmation of the people within my Christian community who said I had a calling on my life. Yet, after nearly five decades, I can say that El Camino was just the beginning. In the 1970s, I ministered through the Renewal Action Programs (RAP) Foundation Services. In the 1980s, I ministered through the Reformed Church in America and its Hispanic Council. Since 1992, I have ministered through the Latino Pastoral Action Center. My experiences through these and other ministries are chronicled in the next four chapters, in which I will share with you the four ways I have ministered — and in which you, too, can minister — in situations of captivity.

CHAPTER 4

You Can Engage Your Community!

⌣*୬ℓ*⌐

In accepting your call to minister in captivity, I hope you echo the prophet Isaiah:

> Also I heard the voice of the Lord, saying, "Whom shall I send, and who will go for us?" Then I said, "Here am I! Send me." (Isaiah 6:8)

Undoubtedly, you are ready to join the struggle and serve. You really do have the unique gifts and talents to make a difference for others and yourself, having been made in God's image. Remember the state of our captive world. You may be free in Christ, but the creation remains in the clutches of captivity (Romans 8:21-22).

As for me, ever since that defining summer over forty-five years ago, I have acted many times on God's call to minister in captivity. Throughout this time, I chose to reject the status quo and agreed to act on my God-given call. When I said yes, God propelled me into his grander plan to reconcile his creation to himself. Along the way, I used my Spirit-given gifts as I carried out and continually adjusted the scope of my ministry in response to the context and the leading of the Spirit. I also involved many people in my ministries, and helped others accept their call and carry out their own ministries.

You too can reject the status quo and act on your God-given call! Indeed, your ministry can reflect your particular context, which God already considered in shaping your specific call. It will include healing, transformation, and celebration, and it very well may include contradictions, confusion, and condemnation, too. You will experience great joy, peace, justice, and victories, sometimes in the midst of unimaginable struggle; but you may not be able to sidestep suffering, frustration, anger, and even bitterness. Still, God will not give you more than you can bear — even if it seems that way at times (1 Corinthians 10:13). Thankfully, negative circumstances do not guarantee failure!

This is what happens when you accept Christ's call to minister in captivity. In the process, you will identify and use your gifts and knowledge as you fulfill your personal plans. You will employ your gifts and knowledge for the common good and teach your knowledge and skills to others. Consequently, you will align your values and beliefs and become impassioned about serving your own community and the larger world. You also will prepare yourself to lead and serve in personal growth and community revitalization efforts and engage others in these efforts. At times, you may even spawn new institutions and collaborative ventures to meet the needs of your community and the society.

As I reflect on my forty-five years of ministering in captivity, I remember many people and structures that were affected by the implications of the Fall, and yet were touched by God's grace. Many people accepted God's call to serve others in a world that was crying out for its freedom from bondage. Together, we engaged others to make a positive difference in the world. We were light and salt. We were catalysts for change. In each ministry, we employed different strategies based on the context and the organic relationships we established with other people and institutions.

All of these incarnational ministries had a common goal — to improve the conditions of people and communities, particularly the historically poor and disenfranchised. At times, I engaged or worked with the powers; at other times, I confronted or challenged them. In addition, I sometimes engaged people and institutions in my community; at other times, I confronted them for exploiting the community. Together, these four approaches, or paradigms, represent the ways I have ministered consistently over time. Of course, one size does not fit all! Your ministry will not look exactly like mine! But it will most likely involve some combination of these four paradigms:

- *Engage Your Community:* When you engage your community, you will establish relationships with people within the covenant community and serve as an instrument of transformation within the church and para-church institutions.

- *Confront Your Community:* When you confront your community, you will call your community to submit to God's will, practice what it professes, and reject unfair doctrines or practices.
- *Engage the Powers:* When you engage the powers, you will establish relationships with people outside of the covenant community and serve as an instrument of transformation within the system and society.
- *Confront the Powers:* When you confront the powers, you will call the powers and principalities to submit to God's plan and his Kingdom and renounce unjust decrees or norms.

As I used each of these approaches, I drew from the examples of different characters in the Old and New Testaments who embodied the different ways of ministering in captivity: Moses, Daniel, Nehemiah, Esther, Mary, John the Baptist, Jesus, Peter, Mary Magdalene, Paul, and so many others. After all these years, I can testify to the fact that our experiences are, in the words of the Apostle Paul, "profitable for doctrine, for reproof, for correction, and for instruction in righteousness, that the man of God may be complete, thoroughly equipped for every good work" (2 Timothy 3:16-17).

Of course, God may not call you to all four paradigms, although he can. The likely scenario is that he will call you to carry out some of them. Nevertheless, he already has placed in your life the people who will help you carry out your call. They may already be in your church and community, or you may meet them when the time is right. Along with these traveling companions, I believe that, as we await the Lord's return, you will be able to contribute immensely to God's total call for his church. You truly can participate in bringing about mature and healthy communities and a responsive society at large.

One final note! You should be aware that some in the church may demonize, discourage, or even dismiss some or all of these paradigms as unimportant or even inappropriate. To them, ministry may mean other things or should be carried out differently. Or it should be based on a different interpretation of Scripture. And you yourself may still have questions about adopting these ministry approaches, perhaps out of fear or lack of experience. Even so, I pray you defer to the Holy Spirit, who has called and equipped you for ministry. I pray the Spirit moves you to integrate what you learn in this book and apply it in your present and future ministries.

Engage Your Community

God calls the church to be a healing community that responds to the spirit, soul, and body needs of the people.[1] As it meets these needs, the church gains the right to be heard and is empowered to lead souls to Christ. The church needs to be a transformational community that reveals glimpses of the Kingdom of God by opposing godless policies and practices; this is how it is light and salt to the earth. This is why you must embrace the church's critical role to seek peace and prosperity, or welfare (shalom), for the larger society.

> And seek the peace [shalom] of the city where I have caused you to be carried away captive, and pray to the LORD for it, for in its peace you will have peace. (Jeremiah 29:5-7)

Of course, you may point to concrete examples of this shalom in local communities, but remember that God's desire is for his *whole creation* to enjoy his glory. This includes urban as much as suburban and rural areas, and poor ones as much as rich ones.

As you engage your community, even to deliver a message of judgment, God calls you to work for your community's restoration. In fact, he may be calling you to be today's Ezekiel, who watches over your people.

> Son of man, I have made you a watchman for the house of Israel; therefore hear a word from my mouth, and give them warning from me. (Ezekiel 3:17)

After Ezekiel cried out to God and sought clarity concerning the fate of God's people (11:13), God told Ezekiel that he ultimately would restore them (11:14-20). Then, Ezekiel returned to his people to tell them what

---

1. When I speak of "community" in this book, I will usually be referring to the Christian community, but you will find that at times I use it to refer to the larger society that includes the Christian community. You may recall from Chapter 2 that when you minister in a situation of captivity, you will interact with the world around you, navigate relationships both within and outside of the Christian community, and work within and outside the systems and structures of our society. The term "community" reflects both present reality as well as the world's future status as a restored part of God's Kingdom. This is why community is described here in light of God's present and ultimate plan to restore and reconcile all things to himself.

God told him (11:25). Later, God informed Ezekiel of his promise to reinstate his covenant with his people (16:59-63).

Of course, Ezekiel could not have understood that an everlasting covenant would come through the perfect atonement in Christ. Yet, he stayed among his people. In the process, he engaged his community to ensure they were not participating in wrongdoing. In fact, God linked Ezekiel's actions to his community's welfare (33:7-8). Thus, Ezekiel's faithfulness to engage his community resulted in deliverance.

In helping Ezekiel restore his people, God encouraged him to be faithful:

> Again, when I say to the wicked, "You shall surely die," if he turns from his sin and does what is lawful and right, if the wicked restores the pledge, gives back what he has stolen, and walks in the statutes of life without committing iniquity, he shall surely live; he shall not die. None of his sins which he has committed shall be remembered against him. He has done what is just and right; he shall surely live. (33:14-16)

Thereafter, Ezekiel became an instrument for the restoration of his people (37:1-14). Toward this end, Ezekiel prophesied to the dry bones; then the Spirit of God breathed life into them. This ensured that God's people would know he was their God (37:20-28). God then told Ezekiel he would free his people from captivity, establish a new covenant with them, and ultimately place them in a new kingdom. Again, while Ezekiel could not have understood that God was pointing to Christ and the Kingdom of God, he still was heartened by God's promise of redemption for the covenant community.

Of course, the covenant community was responsible for seeking the shalom of the overall society (Jeremiah 29:4-7). And while you may not experience the fruit of your labors concerning community building or community development in this lifetime, you still will have contributed to God's plan of restoration. It is in this spirit that you can engage your community. Thus, you can offer spiritual and community ministries. You can make sure to bring about personal and social transformation through your ministry. You also can work collaboratively with others to be light and salt to the society. You can prepare others to help them bring about personal and social transformation. Certainly at least some community members will listen and comply with your efforts, so trust that God will take care of the rest.

Offer Spiritual and Community Ministries

Historically, the body of Christ has divided itself into two main camps: one whose emphasis is on personal piety and one whose focus is on social justice. Personal piety churches tend to advance an agenda centered on morality and so-called "family values," and focus on rugged individualism and personal uprightness. Social justice churches, on the other hand, tend to advance an agenda centered on justice and so-called "human rights," and focus on community development and community organizing. This division has led to one-sided ministry approaches that have contributed to the separation, or dichotomizing, of the sacred and the secular. It also has compartmentalized the private and public dimensions of faith. As a result, it has created an artificial divide, which suggests that family values and morals have nothing to do with human rights; and that justice issues, like poverty and oppression, have nothing to do with morality.

In fact, both sides have overlooked the necessity of the other. Yet the Scriptures are solidly on the side of a holistic response to our captive world, in which one leads a Spirit-filled life *and* engages and confronts fallen powers and principalities. Indeed, there really is no need to dichotomize the sacred and the secular. Jesus himself made this clear upon launching his public ministry:

> The Spirit of the Lord is upon me, because he has anointed me to preach the gospel to the poor. He has sent me to proclaim liberty to the captives and recovery of sight to the blind, to set at liberty those who are oppressed, to proclaim the acceptable year of the Lord. (Luke 4:18-19)

In this holistic approach, Jesus seeks to deal with both the spiritual and social needs of the people, as well as with the behavior and actions of the society toward the people.

From its start, the church institutionalized Christ's holistic example of ministry.

> And they continued steadfastly in the apostles' doctrine and fellowship, in the breaking of bread, and in prayers. Then fear came upon every soul, and many wonders and signs were done through the apostles. Now all who believed were together and had all things in

common, and sold their possessions and goods and divided them among all, as anyone had need. So continuing daily with one accord in the temple and breaking bread from house to house, they ate their food with gladness and simplicity of heart, praising God and having favor with all the people. And the Lord added to the church daily those who were being saved. (Acts 2:42-47)

As you can see here, both spiritual and community components were foundational aspects of the ministry of Christ's church. There was teaching, fellowship, communion, and prayer. There was also community service and community building. This holistic expression resulted in joy and generosity, and led to praising of God and favor from those around them. It also brought about a consistent number of converts to the faith.

In contrast, almost all the learning institutions of the church today (seminaries, Bible colleges, Bible institutes, and so on) have failed to heed Christ's methodology, and thus have perpetuated the dichotomy between the sacred and the secular. Furthermore, the teaching ministries of the local church (Bible studies, Sunday school, discipleship cells, and so forth) also have perpetuated this dichotomy. For this reason, as you minister you will do well to renew existing institutions or to employ new, nontraditional models within and outside the local church, which will prepare people to grow in both their personal and social dimensions.

EL CAMINO PENTECOSTAL CHURCH

In 1965, I became the pastor of El Camino (The Way) Pentecostal Church in Sunset Park, Brooklyn. Before I started, El Camino offered only traditional evangelical ministries that focused on personal conversion: Sunday service, Bible studies, missions, and so on. It did not offer any community programs because such programs were not part of the traditional Pentecostal culture. They were something the church simply did not do. However, I made it clear that I would be involved in the community, as I had seen the need to be involved in the community from early on in my ministry.

As a youth leader at Gospel and Missionary Center, I already had developed a children's program at the church and a drug referral program at a neighboring church. Also, while I attended the Bible Institute in the evenings, I was working as a community worker in the local anti-poverty program. This connected me to financial and human resources that I accessed for the programs at my church and the other local churches.

So, almost immediately, I introduced community ministries at El Camino, which caused the church to begin to interact with the community at large. As a result, the church got involved in the political, educational, and public health issues of the local community. Indeed, the congregation supported my efforts to stand up for peace and justice (social transformation), even though most of its members had previously been predisposed to oppose community involvement. When they expressed concern, I pointed to their individual and collective experiences of being treated unfairly by the system and local residents.

In the midst of engaging the community at large, I felt the duality of living in two worlds — the Kingdom of God and the kingdom of man. In the evening, I would tell the congregation: "Suffer now and your reward will be in heaven. Only God can change things." Then, during the day, I would tell the people with whom I worked, "You do not have to suffer. We can change the system now!" I began to wonder whether the gospel spoke to both worlds. Did the message of Christ speak to our personal situations as well as to our collective situations?

On one occasion, I was arrested for pointing out the inequities that Puerto Ricans faced in the distribution of resources in our community and city. I was one of thirty-seven church leaders arrested at the Board of Estimate in City Hall. Herman Badillo, before he became a congressman or NYC deputy member, represented us. The story even made the evening news. As I was being escorted into the police paddy wagon, I wondered how I would explain my actions to my congregation that night. Would they feel it was appropriate for their pastor to be in handcuffs and arrested? Was this a legitimate role for a man of God, their spiritual leader, their pastor? Later, I learned that one of my older congregants cried when she saw me on the news.

On a gut level, I knew I was doing something right, even though I could not articulate it theologically at the time. So that night, during the evening service, I simply shared with the congregation unapologetically that standing up for the poor and justice was appropriate and that I was proud of it. To my surprise, they were generally supportive. They also admitted that they were not treated fairly by the system. Yet, they were in tension — just as I was — as to whether they or I should get involved directly in combating that injustice. In the end, they accepted that I would continue to be a voice for issues affecting the poor and the marginalized, and that I would be a spiritual leader as well as a community leader.

Thereafter, I continued to preach the Word and offer the traditional evangelical ministries. Yet I also led several community organizations and groups. We held demonstrations on educational and public health issues. We advocated for educational reform and representation of Puerto Ricans in leadership positions. We identified and supported people for elected office. I even became the area's representative to the New York City Council Against Poverty, which connected me to the New York City–wide Puerto Rican and African American leadership. Consequently, the church experienced exponential growth and the lives of many members were transformed.

MELROSE REFORMED CHURCH

With almost a decade of experience engaging in holistic ministry, I became the pastor of the Melrose Reformed Church in the Bronx. Through my involvement with the New York Theological Seminary and mainline denominational circles, I met Rev. Don DeYoung, the pastor of the Elmendorf Reformed Church in East Harlem. He had learned of my growing expertise in urban theological education and transitional ministries, and asked me to consult at Melrose Reformed Church. He believed I had the expertise to revitalize this dying church, so I came for a visit. While Melrose was in a neighborhood that had become predominantly Puerto Rican and black, the twenty or so people I met with were mostly white senior citizens.

After I made my presentation, the church board asked me to become Melrose's full-time pastor and offered me its parsonage and agreed to cover my bills. Up until that time, I had been a part-time pastor and had held a full-time job in the secular world. Nevertheless, it was a difficult decision for me. I worried about the differences between my Pentecostal background and Melrose's Reformed tradition. Would my unapologetic Pentecostal perspective be accepted by the church members? Would my being a staunch advocate of Latino issues be a problem for the predominantly white and African American congregation? Would not having all the advanced degrees and traditional Reformed Church credentials impede my effectiveness? Also, would my own Pentecostal community see me as defecting? I just wasn't sure.

At the same time, I had a general comfort level with being part of interdenominational settings. I was in seminary and my theology was expanding. I was beginning to understand and be open to new possibilities, so I accepted the position. To my surprise, the board allowed me to retain my cultural and religious identity. Yet I cannot tell you that I was completely at ease. I wondered whether I could work within the church's established liturgy and governmental structure. Would I be able to synthesize my personal spiritual formation with the traditional Reformed theology? Would I be accepted by the new South Bronx community, given that I was coming from Brooklyn? In the end, though, I took on the challenge while trusting in God's sovereignty and leading.

Before I started at Melrose, the church offered some traditional community ministries focused on human needs, including an after-school program and an evening teen center. I had directed such programs in previous ministries, and I was attracted to the congregation's comfort with them. But the church had no prayer, Bible study, discipleship, or evangelism ministries. Not surprisingly, they had attracted few neighborhood people who would adopt their worship style and religious experience. When I introduced ministries centered on prayer, evangelism, and other spiritual disciplines, most of the members initially resisted. Very quickly, I understood that I had to help them respond holistically to the social-political-economic-cultural reality of the people by simultaneously addressing their spiritual needs from a Christ-centered evangelical perspective.

As you can guess, my experience at Melrose was comparable to El Camino, only reversed. Of course, by the time I got to Melrose, I was more seasoned than when I was at El Camino. Almost immediately, I integrated a holistic gospel into the congregation. I developed devotional time within the teen center, which had been only recreational up until that point. I also developed a children's chapel in the after-school center. In addition, I changed the church's liturgy and worship style. I preached on both personal and social transformation. I introduced indigenous instruments, including congas, maracas, drums, and tambourines. Members gave personal testimonies, and engaged in street evangelism. I also offered spiritual counseling to the traditional, older, white members of the congregation with deep Reformed roots. In time, the church supported my efforts to instill faithfulness to the rule of God (personal transformation), even though most of the original members had been predisposed to oppose spiritual formation.

Bring about Personal and Social Transformation

As a believer in holistic ministry, I have fought throughout my ministry against the dichotomized, fragmented, and compartmentalized reality of too many churches. Too often I found that churches were not responding to the personal *and* social implications of life. I was sure (and I remain sure!) that God calls us to be instruments of liberation from both personal and collective captivity. As a result, through my ministries, I would seek to bring about both personal and social transformation — transformation of the totality of life.

When I consider the biblical basis for holistic transformation, I turn to the example of the Apostle Peter's transformation. Even though he was a member of the working class, a fisherman, Peter zealously followed Jewish guidelines for personal transformation. We know this from his rejection of the Lord's command to eat food he deemed unclean under Jewish dietary laws (Acts 10:14). Yet, he would experience social transformation when the Lord corrected him for refusing to kill and eat the perceived unclean animal. "What God has cleansed you must not call common" (10:15). We also know this from his resistance to visiting a gentile home (10:28). When Jesus sent him to the home of Cornelius, a Roman centurion, Peter realized that he had to preach to and accept into the body of Christ people whom he used to socially ostracize (10:44-48).

Here, Peter's experiential reality proved foundational for his theological reflection and formation. His personal experience of the vision and with Cornelius resulted in his acceptance of Cornelius and the other gentiles in his house. This led to the shift in his theological direction wherein he accepted gentiles into the body of Christ. Indeed, Peter's social transformation can be seen fully when he advocated the full inclusion of gentiles into Christ's body during his presentation to the Jewish council (Acts 15).

Not surprisingly, I see the church as being responsible for lifting up its members to carry out God's work for people, the church, and the society. Yet many church members are locked into a negative mindset, believing the lies of the world that they do not have the potential or the necessary knowledge and skills to do it. As a result, the church must undo years of the system's conditioning and of its own internalized attitudes, which often limit believers' ability and potential. As a believer, you have to believe in yourself. You have to increase your self-worth.

You have to refrain from being defined by the system's criteria and recognize that both you and others have a lot of expertise from your own practical ministries.

Regrettably, the church has not always provided many opportunities for its members to become holistic. Too often, members do not acquire the knowledge or skills to carry out holistic ministry. The desire to serve may be present, but the capacity to carry it out usually is not developed. Also, the lack of adequate infrastructure among churches and their ministries has resulted in few or no spaces to operate and teach holistic ministry. This has created frustration and tension within the churches and their ministries.

Consequently, through my ministries, I worked hard to equip individuals to be aligned with the vision of holistic ministry. Toward this end, I preached the Word through chapel services, special events, and community outreaches. I also involved members of my congregation in leadership institutes, conferences, seminars, and workshops, individual and group counseling, and mentoring. Some people I ministered to went on to start their own holistic ministries in areas such as mental health, environmental justice, HIV/AIDS, youth empowerment, international missions, and community development. These individuals integrated pastoral and prophetic ministries by ministering to individual needs and working for systemic change.

When I consider the potential for people to be holistic, I recall the story of Paul's (or Saul's) conversion, his famous "Damascus experience" (Acts 9). How did Paul transform from his zealous, blameless, pharisaical life to being, in his own words, the chief of all sinners (1 Timothy 1:15)? And how did he understand this as a good thing? Of course, God transformed Paul's personal life in that he had found his Messiah. Yet God also transformed his social life in that Paul went from being a strict observer of ritual purity laws to one who accepted the "heathen, pagan, unclean" gentiles, people he had once disdained. Paul developed social relationships with them and integrated them into the life of the covenant community. God transformed him into the Apostle to the Gentiles: "And when James, Cephas, and John, who seemed to be pillars, perceived the grace that had been given to me, they gave me and Barnabas the right hand of fellowship, that we should go to the Gentiles and they to the circumcised" (Galatians 2:9).

RENEWAL ACTION PROGRAMS (RAP)
FOUNDATION SERVICES

At the start of my ministry career, I did not have a clear understanding of holistic ministry. But I was aware enough to found the Renewal Action Programs (RAP) Foundation Services in Sunset Park, Brooklyn. It was the late 1960s. I was still the pastor of El Camino, but I opened this faith-based, multi-service ministry to reach the broader community. Through the RAP Family Service Center, we provided case management to welfare recipients, housing support, high school equivalency, and English as a second language classes. We also provided services to the families of the youth program participants. Rev. Pedro Windsor was the director, and then minister A. David Anglada was the associate director.

These two young ministers were open to nontraditional ministry, so I educated them about holistic ministry in the context of servicing the clients of the center. I pointed out how the Scriptures revealed that spiritual and community work was all part of Christian ministry. Minister Anglada had come from a more traditional evangelistic preaching setting, while Rev. Windsor had been working for a community ministry that focused on electoral politics. Thereafter, they prayed for and anointed people. They advocated on behalf of people in various systems. They also dealt with federal, state, city, and local government, including the local community planning board. Many times, they organized and demonstrated against the community planning board, particularly when it did not want to approve community programs or tried to defund them.

As we looked at our struggles to sustain our community programs, we recognized that we had to expand our focus to the social arena. This prompted us to get involved in the local political arena. There was a lot of tension in Sunset Park. Ethnic and racial conflict was everywhere. The Puerto Rican community was growing, and the white community felt threatened. The challenges by the white community were becoming so strong that we decided to become involved in local electoral politics. So, we chose the most vulnerable government position, which was held by a female district leader, and selected Antonia "Tony" Cabán to run for that office.

I convinced her that this did not contradict RAP's holistic ministry vision. The Bible gave her permission to run for office, I said, pointing to the many political leaders from the covenant community in the Bible: kings, prophets, and judges, including Deborah, a female judge. I maintained that she would be a legitimate voice for the community. After we prayed about it, she accepted the charge. If she had won, she would have committed to engage and confront the powers to ensure that the powers were responding to the needs of her constituents.

Even though we were inexperienced in electoral politics, it was an incredible experience! It was the first attempt by the Puerto Rican community of Sunset Park to win an electoral seat. We recruited people to collect petitions, organized the petitions, and sealed the petitions. The political machine tried to knock us off the ballot, but we organized a grassroots campaign that kept Tony on the ballot. We sought the direction and gained the support of the local churches, telling them how important it would be for an elected official who had Christian values to be in the system. We also galvanized the Latino community, and it became a major effort in the Sunset Park community.

Throughout, we constantly reflected and debated about how God was involved in our holistic efforts to engage the community and the powers. In the end, we lost the election, but the experience was valuable. The community that had been against us knew it could no longer take us for granted. This effort opened the eyes and doors for other Latinos to hold elected office. That campaign was the beginning and it laid a solid foundation. Forty-five years later, we have two Latino local elected officials in Sunset Park, the NYS assemblyman and NYC councilwoman. Of course, we continued to seek the personal and social transformation of the community through RAP's Family Service Center.

LATINO PASTORAL ACTION CENTER

Decades later, in the early 1990s, after having served in a string of secular posts, I had a vision to launch another full-time holistic ministry that would address personal and social issues affecting people and institutions, particularly in low-income communities of color. I began by reflecting on the conditions of people, institutions, the community, and the society. Then I developed a realistic and ambitious plan to respond to that reality. It was at this same time that I began writing down the theology of captivity I had been developing over the years, as well as the principles and beliefs and strategy of my holistic ministry vision. This, I felt confident, would provide the proper foundation from which to take action and bear much fruit.

My return to full-time ministry meant that I would be the primary interpreter and implementer of the vision that God had birthed in me. I would be its central guide. I would proclaim and apply a holistic gospel, which would seek to reconcile the personal with the social, the individual with the collective. Its vision, mission, strategy, and programs and services would address the totality of human existence. It would respond simultaneously to people's quest for a relationship with their creator and to their pursuit of relationship with themselves, their neighbors, and the environment.

Because I was committed to doing holistic ministry, I decided not to be employed by any organization or system that ultimately could control the substance or message of my vision. I put a fleece before the Lord, asking for one of three ministries. First, I could become the pastor of a large congregation with multi-pastoral staff, which would allow me to implement holistic ministries. Second, I could become the executive director of a large community-based organization that addressed the needs of my community, which he would allow me to shape into a holistic ministry. Third, I could be the founder of a new holistic ministry that would provide both spiritual and community services.

God responded providentially through the Hispanic Initiative at the Pew Charitable Trusts. One of my ministry peers, Rev. Benjamin Alicea, told me about Pew's newly formed Hispanic Initiative and its director, Rev. Danny Cortes, with whom he had a personal relationship. Ben set up an initial meeting for me, and I made a presentation to Danny, who encouraged me to submit a proposal. My concept of ministry was exactly the kind of project that Pew wanted to fund. So in 1992 I launched the Latino Pastoral Action Center (LPAC) as a NYC-based, Christ-centered, faith-based organization. Later, I leveraged additional funding from the New York Foundation and the Aaron Diamond Foundation. Together with Pew, they became LPAC's founding funders.

From 1992 through 1996, LPAC was a division of the NYC Mission Society, the oldest private social services agency in New York City. Then, after four years of success and growth, it became an independent organization. In 1997, the Mission Society gifted LPAC its City Mission Cadet Corps building in the Highbridge neighborhood of the Bronx, to serve as LPAC's headquarters. That same year, LPAC changed the building's name to the Urban Ministry Complex and began offering holistic services to the local community and the city, and eventually the nation and several countries in Latin America.

From its inception, LPAC operated several local and citywide holistic ministries. Led by Rev. David Ramos, and later Rev. Hiram Ríos and Rev. Carlos Garcia, we operated the Urban Youth Fellows Leadership Program from 1994 until 2000 for over 150 urban youth leaders who worked predominately with Latino and black youth, and many established or worked in holistic ministries in NYC and across the country. Led by Rev. Elizabeth Ríos, we ran the Center for Emerging Female Leadership (CEFL) from 1994 through 2003, to serve women who were emerging or established leaders in church or society. CEFL grew out of Latinas in Ministry, which had been led by Dr. María Pérez y González.

From the Urban Ministry Complex, hundreds of children grades K-6 have been served through the New Hope after-school program, receiving homework help, tutoring, physical fitness activities, cultural awareness, and leadership development. Through the Greater Heights youth program, thousands of youth ages 14-21 participated in SAT prep, academic and college advisement, college trips, sports clinics and teams, and support and leadership clubs. Both of these programs were led by my son, Esteban Rivera. He also ran the Latin America Missions Project, LAMP, which took youth and young adults to short-term mission projects in Honduras, Cuba, and the Dominican Republic. Esteban created LAMP as part of the Urban Youth Fellows Leadership Program.

From 1998 through 2003, we provided these programs through our AmeriCorps Urban Ministry Project, which was led by my daughter, Susana Rivera León, now LPAC's vice president. The project enabled as many as thirty community residents per year to serve their communities and engage residents in service and revitalization projects. Some went on to become teachers at our Family Life Academy Charter School and full-time members at LPAC and other community-based organizations. Of particular note was Mandi Martinez, who launched our First Steps Daycare Center as an AmeriCorps member and served as the director for its first eight years. Today, First Steps serves as many as fifty children, ages 2-6, in our second site.

On a community level, we offered a program called Nuestra Gente (Our People). Started in 1998 under the leadership of Juan Rodríguez-Muñóz, Nuestra Gente organized, developed, and assisted engagement in the local electoral, educational, political, and community processes. Residents received leadership skills training and became prepared to take collective action to improve their neighborhood. Through Nuestra Gente, we became the community sponsor of over twelve homes (called

Villas de Paz) in the Southwest Bronx. We also were involved with the South Bronx Development Corporation, and produced a neighborhood study to bring about local redevelopment.

On the educational front, we secured a charter school license under the State of New York Alternative School Program and launched the Family Life Academy Charter School in 2001. While a separate legal entity, the school is the product of LPAC's guidance, vision, and hard work and is one of the most important building blocks for community empowerment that LPAC has undertaken. The high-performing K-8 school is housed at LPAC's headquarters and helps children to achieve high standards, take responsibility for their own learning, and explore and affirm human values. My wife, Marilyn Calo Rivera, was the principal for eight years.

To serve local populations in crisis, we also partnered with other service-providing institutions. In 2002, we launched the Temporary Assistance for Needy Families Program to conduct outreach and social services for eligible families who had been sanctioned and were in jeopardy of losing their Public Assistance benefits. We successfully located the families, registered them, taught them job readiness skills, and assisted them with job placement. Our results exceeded the milestones set by NYC Human Resources Administration.

From 2002 through 2005, we secured a subcontract from Narco Freedom to operate Liberation Manor, a transitional residence for homeless persons afflicted and affected by HIV/AIDS and substance abuse. First led by Rev. William Reyes and then by Rev. Percy Howard, we provided a safe and secure environment for up to sixty daily residents. We provided in-house individual and group counseling, and made referrals to psychological and psychiatric consultations, social service agencies, and job training programs. We also provided referrals to neighboring churches for pastoral counseling. We provided chaplaincy services in conjunction with volunteer churches and faith-based groups. We also offered a daily breakfast program at our partner's site, the Fellowship Chapel. We also partnered with the NYC shelter system for the homeless.

From 2005 until 2007, we partnered again with Narco Freedom to operate the House of Healing, a residential transformation center for men seeking liberation from captivity to substance abuse. Led first by Rev. William Reyes and then Rev. Alfred Correa, we provided in-house individual and group counseling, and made referrals to psychological and psychiatric consultations, social service agencies, and job training programs. We also provided referrals to neighboring churches for pastoral counseling. In addition, we created and supervised work experience opportunities within and outside the facilities.

In a similar light, we ran the Fatherhood Initiative from 2003 through 2007 and helped over two hundred men become holistic fathers. Under the leadership of Rev. José Carlos Montes and then Rev. William Reyes, the men participated in weekly individual and group counseling and a life skills–building Fathers' Circle. In the process, they dealt with their own issues while receiving tangible strategies for how to be a positive light in their children's lives. Scores of men reestablished relationships with their children and their children's mothers. Others increased their engagement and availability with their children. Many began to provide financial, material, and emotional support to their sons and daughters. Many also reconciled with their wives or girlfriends.

All told, LPAC facilitated the growth and development of thousands of children, youth, and adults. Through our holistic, servant-leadership development model, countless individuals became holistic, and thus helped shift their community's paradigm to personal and social responsibility. In the process, they have become leaders with strong, socially minded character. They have become peacemakers, literate (effective communicators), successful in school and work, physically fit, arts-oriented, engaged in their family life, active in community affairs, and mentors to their peers or younger individuals. Many have worked to strengthen the Four Pillars of Community Life.

Among the successes are stronger and more stable families; schools with high student performance and more parental involvement; a high number of high school and higher education enrollments and completions; lower incidence of crime and local safety corridors; increased leadership in school, community, and religious congregation groups; greater participation in community revitalization and building projects; increased volunteerism and financial support for community revitalization efforts; and scores of youth and adult mentors caring for the needs of their peers or younger individuals.

Work Collaboratively to Be Light and Salt

At this point, I could be dishonest and claim that my ministry has been a one-man show. But I can hardly count how many people have been my traveling companions. Regrettably, not everyone has shared my spirit of collaboration. Yet the church would do well to avoid the division that plagues it and its associated ministries. If it did, the artificial walls of separation would fall. Churches would relate to one another and even share power. People would be accepted beyond tokenism or being objects of mission and dependence. They would be included as builders, not simply as beneficiaries of services or resources. Territorial issues would vanish. *Who belongs to whom?* would be replaced with, *How can we have interdenominational and intercouncil cooperation?* The church would establish new institutional expressions and even collaborate in response to the prevailing needs of Christians and the society at large.

What makes collaboration essential is that God closely ties the success, and even survival, of his people to the actions of individual members toward the larger community. Throughout history, God's most effective collaborators engaged people within their communities. Frederick Douglass, Charles Grandison Finney, and Lucretia Mott were connected to other abolitionists, former slaves, and slaves. Susan B. Anthony and Martha Wright were connected to other women fighting for the right to vote. Rev. Dr. Martin Luther King Jr. was connected to the black church, and African American people and institutions, all of which were fighting for civil rights. More recently, Jim Wallis and Rev. Luis Cortes are connected to immigrant advocates and immigrants.

These and so many others have been intimately connected to their people. While carrying out their individual functions, they have sought out and maintained strong ties and direct relationships with their communities, which were in situations of captivity. They also took the opportunities to share their faith and build relationships that would eventually facilitate the liberation struggle of their people. Indeed, the Scriptures showed them how to represent their people collaboratively.

For example, Joseph provided for his family in the midst of the Egyptian famine (Genesis 45:16-24); he also brought his family to Egypt with the support of the Pharaoh (46:5-7). He did these things even though his brothers had sold him into slavery in Egypt during his youth. Joseph understood that his connection to his people was directed by God, which guided him to recognize the responsibility he had to ensure their welfare.

> "But as for you, you meant evil against me; but God meant it for good, in order to bring it about as it is this day, to save many people alive. Now therefore, do not be afraid; I will provide for you and your

little ones." And he comforted them and spoke kindly to them. (50:20-21)

Indeed, Joseph's collaborative spirit must have been fed by the realization of the vision he received from God in his youth.

In contrast, Esther in Persia needed help to tap into her collaborative spirit. After Esther became queen, she would meet regularly with her uncle, Mordecai, who sought to learn how she was doing and what was happening with her (Esther 2:11). Yet, after she learned that Mordecai was suffering due to a harmful decree ordering the genocide of God's covenant community, Queen Esther offered insufficient relief to the grieving Mordecai (4:4). When Mordecai challenged her response, Esther cited Persian law to explain why she could not address the king in time to change the law (4:11).

Through Esther's eunuch, Mordecai informed Esther that her address to the king was instrumental to the success, the survival, of the covenant community:

> And Mordecai told them to answer Esther: "Do not think in your heart that you will escape in the king's palace any more than all the other Jews. For if you remain completely silent at this time, relief and deliverance will arise for the Jews from another place, but you and your father's house will perish. Yet who knows whether you have come to the kingdom for such a time as this?" (Esther 4:13-14)

Indeed, Esther's silence would have contributed to the demise of her lineage. But she ultimately recognized God's higher purpose and plan for her life. She then resolved to face the king on behalf of the community even at the personal risk of death: "And so I will go to the king, which is against the law; and if I perish, I perish!" (4:16). Afterward, she collaborated with Mordecai and her community by mobilizing her people inside and outside the palace, thus tying her fate to that of her community.

ASSOCIATION OF SUNSET PARK PASTORS

From the beginning of my ministry, I recognized the power of working together with others for the benefit of the larger community and society. I also understood that I could not always wait for community members to arrive at this conclusion on their own. So, while at El Camino, I faced a Pentecostal culture that was against offering community programs. But I wanted to run community programs, even though I did not have the necessary resources. I could have gone outside my community and collaborated with other groups. I easily could have become the spokesperson, or token, for my community in those coalitions. And while this intercultural collaboration is necessary, too, I accepted the challenge to organize within my own community. I wanted our community to have power in its own right. For this, I committed to establish a power base within our people.

So I went to the other local ministers and developed the Association of Sunset Park Pastors to help me secure these resources. The pastor of the largest Assemblies of God church in Sunset Park responded. He was a respected figure and was considered the area's godfather. I knew that if he was involved, others would follow. He agreed, and the association was born. With the support of this collective of Sunset Park Pentecostal churches, I went to the local anti-poverty program. The powers knew the churches were behind me, so they awarded the association a grant to operate a summer day camp. The camp was housed at El Camino; the counselors came from other churches, and the director came from the Assemblies of God church.

The program was a success, serving over a hundred children. It was the first time a local Pentecostal church had received a grant. It also was the first time that my community had engaged the powers, which created a presence for our segment of the community. Thus, while our constituents may have been ambivalent at the start, and we may have been ahead of them because of our vision and clarity, they came along — even if it was with kicking and screaming. In many ways, their support of the summer day camp laid the groundwork for their future individual and denominational work in the larger community.

ACCIÓN CÍVICA EVANGÉLICA

Thankfully, my experience with collaboration proved easier several years later in the early 1970s when I took advantage of two factors that culminated in the development of the citywide Acción Cívica Evangélica (Civic Evangelical Action). The first was the phenomenal growth of storefront Pentecostal churches, which had grown to as many as two thousand churches. The second was the relationship I established with Joseph Erazo, the director of Hispanic affairs under NYC Mayor Abraham Beame. I told him about the collective leadership of the Pentecostal church, and he approached me about the resources that were available to combat poverty.

Immediately I convened a meeting of leaders from Pentecostal and other denominational churches. I involved Methodists, Disciples of Christ, Lutherans, Evangelicals, Baptists, and Pentecostals. I raised the importance of the church to provide community services. I also stressed the need to engage and confront the city's administration because it was not being responsive to the Puerto Rican community. So we formed Acción Cívica Evangélica. Then, through Mr. Erazo's advocacy, we accessed city funding, which enabled us to offer developmental services to people of all ages. Within a few years, Acción had become the largest evangelical Pentecostal social service group in New York City.

Thousands of young people participated in our summer youth employment program, particularly through our summer lunch program. Adults participated in our workforce program. Senior citizens were part of our seniors program. We even engaged young pastors, seminarians, and recent college graduates to navigate the intricacies of the governmental bureaucracies, and prepared them to oversee program monitoring, reporting, and evaluating requirements. Before we knew it, we were administering a budget of millions of dollars. We moved into two floors on 22nd Street and Park Avenue to house our staff of nearly forty people. We had grown at such a fast pace, which brought with it an immense responsibility. Suddenly we were the subject of news stories, being charged with organizing into a bloc. Other religious institutions, like Catholic Charities and Jewish groups, also took notice of us.

At the same time, we experienced challenges because we did not understand the governmental bureaucracies, or the monitoring, reporting, and evaluating that was involved for each agency. So we solicited the help of young pastors, seminarians, and recent college graduates, who staffed these positions. I am amazed how many of them are now Ph.D.s, mature pastors and ministers, and leaders of their own organizations. Forty years after these seeds were planted, fruit is still being borne.

PROJECT LIBERTY:
BEACON OUTREACH NEW YORK

Several decades later, through LPAC, I launched Project Liberty: Beacon Outreach New York, a citywide outreach and crisis counseling program for individuals, families, and groups affected by the September 11 tragedy. Through Project Liberty, we established a partnership of eight churches and a mental health center: Latino Pastoral Action Center, Urban Youth Alliance International, and Love Gospel Assembly in the Bronx; Resurrection Church and Bayridge Christian Center in Brooklyn; Harlem's Bethel Gospel Assembly and New York City Link in Manhattan; and Bethel Gospel Tabernacle in Jamaica, Queens. These were influential churches that had networks of their own. They also were geographically situated in such a way that they could help us reach out to a great many NYC residents.

At the time, the NYC Department of Mental Health and Hygiene had contracted several community-based organizations and mental health centers to serve community members needing counseling. However, they were not generating the expected number of clients. I was approached by Jewish psychologist and community practitioner Dr. Allen Goodwin of New York City Link, who knew I had a relationship with Mental Health and Hygiene. He and I agreed that LPAC would be the partnership's lead agency. For my part, I was looking forward to this initiative because it could show that the church had access and could make inroads in the local community. We would share sound mental health services, and we would establish and build bridges within the community.

Led by Rev. Elizabeth Ríos, Project Liberty had a multicultural and interracial staff of over 100 people. Its central office was in the Bronx, and it had eight hubs in the Bronx, Brooklyn, Manhattan, and Queens. Each site hired its own people, with our final approval. In turn, the central office provided materials, held weekly staff meetings, and monitored outreach. In the initial months following the tragedy, we processed over 450 individuals who had lost jobs, under the auspices of World Vision. Then, each hub connected with an average of 7,500 participants through the project partners and the local neighborhoods. In the end, we served over 60,000 NYC residents.

Indeed, Project Liberty proved to foster collaboration beyond the original partnership. All told, we connected with nineteen other NYC churches, community-based organizations, and mental health centers, including Full

Circle Health, Bethel Educational Center, Daytop Village, Good Neighborhood Senior Center, New York Christian Resource Center, Franklin Street Kids, Buena Vida Nursing Home, Mission of Mercy, Betances Clinic, North General Hospital, Beth Hark in Harlem, Salvation Army, Highbridge Advisory Council, Vehicles, YMCA, Staten Island Mental Health, Healthy Connections, NYC Immigration Coalition, and Safe Horizons.

Prepare Others to Bring about
Personal and Social Transformation

Indeed, Project Liberty started me back on the path to helping other groups establish holistic ministries to bring about personal and social transformation. From 1992 to 1996, I had operated through LPAC the Holistic Ministry Leadership Institute, the Individual Servant Training Program, and, in conjunction with the Fundraising School of the Indiana University Center of Philanthropy, the Fundraising Institute; Urban Youth Fellows Leadership Program; and Association of Church-based Community Ministries. Then, in 1997, when LPAC moved to the Urban Ministry Complex, I also incubated several faith and community-based organizations: Rev. Olga Torres Simpson's Angels Unaware, Rev. Wendy Calderón-Payne's Urban Youth Alliance, and Rev. Rosa Caraballo's Bruised Reed Ministry.

Over the years, I found many churches resistant to efforts to address both the personal and social dimensions of holistic ministry. The personal piety churches would not employ opportunities for the social dimensions (peace and justice issues) of the faith. On the other hand, the social justice churches would not employ opportunities for the personal dimensions (faithfulness to the rule of God). *It's too overwhelming,* one church says. *The issues are too great,* says another. *We don't have the expertise or know the language to act or speak on these matters.*

Yet many churches have addressed the personal and social dimensions of ministry more than they have recognized. They did not use the same language or employ a framework that clearly showed they were experientially holistic. Nevertheless, I have seen so often in the Latino Pentecostal evangelical community that the churches condemn immoral behavior, but are then the first to open their individual homes to these "immoral" people. They create makeshift detox rooms in their homes to help heal a drug addict — without calling it ministry. They condemn dealing with the systems and structures of the world, but then call for or even accompany those who are being mistreated by a system or structure of the powers — without calling it advocacy.

In working with churches all these years, I also have found that churches often do not provide mentoring opportunities, and definitely not ones that are both structured and relational. Most churches employ a structured, corporate model, which tends to be impersonal. In such environments, mentoring relationships tend to deteriorate into professional relationships. The mentees "learn the business," but they do not get to know their mentors in all their humanity. In contrast, churches that employ a relaxed, relational approach tend to be too personal. Often these experiences deteriorate into loose friendships, with few interactions with the mentor's professional life. Not surprisingly, mentees did not gain much from their mentors' ministry expertise in either situation.

When churches have provided formal training opportunities, I have found that most have limited the people who could benefit from these learning spaces. Most formal educational institutions involve select individuals, which leaves the vast majority of people without the kind of advanced knowledge that will increase their effectiveness in ministry. These spaces have rarely established alternative teaching spaces within their walls, or have supported external venues in which people could receive and apply information in their ministry settings. What's more, in many of these settings, there often has been no diversity among the instructors, which can lead to the belief that some groups are unable to learn or carry out holistic ministry.

Even when educational spaces are available, they do not always provide enough practical ways to learn the materials. The prevailing teaching methodologies tend to be theoretical, and people are expected to test their acquired knowledge and skills in real-life situations without the benefit of testing them in safe, nurturing simulated spaces. Educational institutions also have rarely equipped people with formal ministry plans or implementation strategies. Too often, even when teaching spaces have offered hands-on learning opportunities, they have not necessarily employed advanced educators or practitioners, who could provide significant insights.

Furthermore, I have found that churches have not always made their spaces available to other faith and community groups to carry out their peace and justice work. Affordable space is at a premium for faith and community groups. Unfortunately, many churches use their space for what they term "spiritual" endeavors on Sundays, and close for most weekdays. While many nonprofit and community groups are working for change, many churches have not opened their doors to such groups, regardless of whether they are aligned with the church's mission or with Kingdom values. To do so would increase credibility and good will for churches within the community. It also would enable churches to provide spiritual reflections that are rooted in peace and justice, and would lift up the holistic message for faith and secular groups. However, too many have failed to rise to the occasion and get connected to the broader peace and justice movements in their community.

Interestingly, the Scriptures reflect an ongoing strategic effort by Jesus and his disciples to prepare others to bring about personal and social transformation. The gospel mission and mandate was always meant to be taken to the whole world (Acts 1:8), a task which could not be accomplished by a small group like the original twelve disciples. From the very beginnings of the church, we see the concrete holistic leadership models of Peter, John, James, and Paul. Peter instructed the churches of the Diaspora. John exhorted the churches in Asia Minor based on his experiential apocalyptic vision. Paul gave specific instructions to the leaders he developed, including Timothy, Titus, Philemon, Mark, and so on.

In particular, these leaders provided leadership and transformation principles, both to those who were near them and to those who were no longer in their immediate presence. They did this through their writings and by convening meetings and councils in which they shared their theological considerations, and evaluated and reflected upon them. This provided subsequent direction as to the mission of the church. It was crucial to the identity of the church and how it was supposed to be understood by its new adherents. Those who learned went on to carry out the implications of their specific callings and subsequently were situated all around the world of that time.

Paul certainly dealt with the question of how believers should live personally. For instance, he told Timothy to be an example to other believers and other leaders and churches (1 Timothy 4:12). His instructions contained social aspects as well, as when he told the Corinthian Christians that they were not to let the courts of the Roman Empire judge their disputes, nor eat food that had been sacrificed to Roman gods and festivals (1 Corinthians 8). Certainly, these instructions went beyond personal piety and had direct social implications for the people who heard them.

James instructed people who had been exiled on how to deal with the social issues of poverty and class, and he taught them about the interconnection of salvation and the work of the ministry. He challenged the wealthy in the church not to base their relations on their socioeconomic status, even to the point of stating that it was a disadvantage to them if they were not sensitive to the poor and oppressed among them (James 2). He warned them that God would denounce them if they were not just in their relationship to workers (5:4). He also warned them against worldliness (4:4) and judgment toward others (4:11).

In Revelation, John wrote to individuals and the leaders of the seven churches in Asia (Revelation 2–3). In apocalyptic language, John described for the Christians of that era some of the personal, social, and political happenings of his time. He talked about the interplay between religious, political, and economic systems, and how they impacted the church and the larger society.

Given the biblical mandate to adopt and apply the vision of holistic ministry, I committed part of my ministry to equip churches and community-based organizations to bring about personal and social transformation. Over the years, I have served hundreds of faith-based and community-based organizations throughout the United States, Latin America, and the Caribbean, in such places as California, Florida, Illinois, Massachusetts, New Jersey, New York, Pennsylvania, Puerto Rico, Cuba, Dominican Republic, Honduras, and Venezuela. I entered these relationships knowing that the people and institutions I was working with already possessed the building blocks to impact their social-economic-political-religious reality. My objective simply was to help them employ holistic strategies, which would enable them to engage people and systems and structures, and thus improve the conditions in their communities and the social fabric of the society.

Throughout my ministry, I have been a catalyst regarding several movements that influenced the church. First, when I began my ministry I articulated that preaching should not be relegated to a message of eternal life, abundant life in the present, and forgiveness of personal and individual sin. It also should address the spiritual, social, economic, political, and cultural realities of our communities. No longer should the church teach a dichotomized gospel, one that addressed the personal or the social at the expense of the other. As a result, many of my generation's peers included the ramifications and consequences of corporate and institutional sin in their preaching and teaching.

Second, I modeled a ministry life that was not exclusionary, legalistic, or ethnocentric. I strived to show the possibility of an alternative way of doing ministry — one that blended the best of the indigenous church with the universal church. Consequently, I welcomed Christians from other backgrounds to serve through my ministries, as well as to speak to our constituents through urban missions, special events, and exchanges. I accomplished this without compromising my ability to engage Christian brothers and sisters in dialogue that dealt with the historical and contemporary oppression inflicted by the institutional dominant church.

Third, by establishing a holistic ministry model, I helped shift the traditional thinking that God's power, love, and mercy could only be demonstrated through word and sacrament ministries. Indeed, a Christian community development model could also reflect God's love and the Kingdom values of peace and justice. I showed people that we should not only be concerned with personal piety, as characterized by ministries that focus on personal issues like drug addiction, alcoholism, and sexual abstinence.

We also should address the systemic and underlying causes of these sins. Holistic ministries engage the culture in a way that challenges the culture to submit to God's ultimate Kingdom values. In fact, we have a *responsibility* to influence the culture, the lifestyle, the ethos of the society. The ministries I was a part of inspired a new generation of Christian individuals and institutions to adopt and apply a holistic model of ministry. Consequently, many have been challenging the individual and institutional expressions of the gospel that do not address the whole person — both within and outside the church.

Finally, I shifted my focus from being the only indigenous voice within dominant cultural institutions to helping develop indigenous institutions. At first I felt tension about doing this, because there still was an urgent need for indigenous voices within institutions of the dominant society. But then I recommended other indigenous voices to join these institutions and advised them on how to maximize their role within these institutions. Subsequently, along with my ministry partner Rev. José Carlos Montes, I began to educate, equip, and empower Latino and other urban churches to develop holistic ministries through a variety of leadership development and capacity-building services. In the process, hundreds of churches, faith-based organizations, and secular community-based organizations adopted and applied our Christ-centered community development strategy.

LPAC Capacity Building and
Leadership Development Services

Drawing from my experience with Project Liberty and my previous initiatives, we provided holistic leadership development and capacity building services through partnerships. This way, I directly reflected the learning I had gained. In 2004, we launched the AmeriCorps National Urban Ministry Project, a capacity-building and direct service partnership of five faith-based organizations: LPAC in the Bronx; Ayuda Community Center in Philadelphia; La Capilla del Barrio in Chicago; My Friend's House in Whittier, California; and Spanish Evangelical Church in Lawrence, Massachusetts. We provided technical assistance and guidance to ensure formal and informal connections and shared learning opportunities among the sites. In turn, our partners developed programs and activities for children, youth, and adults, along with corresponding paperwork and assessment tools.

From 2005 through 2007, we operated the National Holistic Ministry Development Project in New York and Chicago. In Chicago, we were represented skillfully by Rev. Pedro Windsor, who you may recall worked with me at RAP Foundation Services in Sunset Park. For the past thirty years, he has been the pastor of La Capilla del Barrio (the Neighborhood Church) in Chicago's Humboldt Park neighborhood. During this time, Pedro has been an outstanding advocate of holistic ministry, having balanced the spiritual and community needs of the city and its people. In New York, Rev. Juan Carlos Morales helped lead the charge. Through both sites, we provided training and technical assistance to nearly two hundred faith-based and community-based organizations in the two sites. We also awarded and monitored sub-awards to over thirty partners, totaling over $280,000.

From 2007 through 2009, we operated the Transforming Youth Capacity Building Project, a three-year capacity-building and leadership development initiative that assisted faith-based and community-based organizations in developing youth servant leaders around the issues of gang prevention, youth violence, and child abuse/neglect. Along with our own Greater Heights Youth Program, we partnered with four other NYC youth-serving organizations: CitiVision (Washington Heights/Inwood in Manhattan), Generation Xcel (Lower East Side in Manhattan), Infinity Church (Soundview in the Bronx), and the Coalition of Youth Workers (citywide).

Along with our consultant, Jeremy Del Rio, we trained our partners in holistic ministry operations, organizational development, community engagement, leadership development, and fund development. We also awarded our partners sub-awards totaling over $75,000 for fundraising systems (in-house and online), websites, youth boards, client tracking system, and so forth. Through the project, the partners also engaged in several collaborations, including the 20/20 Vision Adopt-a-School initiative.

From 2007 through 2008, we operated the Bronx Capacity Building Project, a capacity-building and leadership development initiative that targeted Bronx faith-based and community-based organizations. For this initiative, we partnered with eight NYC organizations: Chapel Youth Ministries, Iglesia de Dios El Refugio, Inc., Learning Disabilities Support Center of New York, One Family Community Center, Orange County Prison Ministry, Survival Instinct — The Network, Inc., Truth at John 14:6, and United Auto Merchants Association. Every partner was trained in holistic ministry development and operations, leadership development, and fund development.

From 2008 until 2009, we operated the Youth Service and Capacity Project, a capacity-building and leadership development initiative that assisted faith-based and community-based organizations serving out-of-school youth. We partnered with five NYC organizations serving out-of-school youth: The Community Shop, Inc.; Opening Doors, Healing Wounds; Rahab's House; Success is Mine; and the United Federation of Evangelical Youth. Every partner was trained in holistic ministry development, holistic ministry operations (focusing on services to out-of-school youth), organizational development, community engagement, leadership development (of board, staff, and volunteers), and fund development.

In addition to the capacity building and leadership development services, in the last few years, we have also incubated several faith-based and community-based organizations in the Urban Ministry Complex. Led by my son Joel Ray Rivera, Servicing Our Youth is a youth civic engagement program that develops youth community decision-makers. Led by Israel Rodríguez, the American Latin Association of New York is a mentoring program for middle school youth. Led by Pedro Estevez, the United Auto Merchants Association is a network that serves small and mid-sized auto merchants. Survival Instinct — The Network, Inc., provides cancer awareness and advocacy.

As I have engaged my community locally and nationally, I have come across many people who have received some type of support from me and subsequently formed ministries of their own. I am humbled by their expressions of gratitude. Some recall times when I held their hands as I took them to their first funder. Others recall a teaching or a nugget that they incorporated in their ministries. They remarked on my openness to share my learnings and resources so they could launch their ministries. I was just happy to serve them and watch them serve others. By sharing these experiences, I hope I have helped you envision ways that God may be calling you to engage your community.

CHAPTER 5

You Can Confront Your Community!

⚮

While I look back warmly at the moments of unity I shared with you in the last chapter, I also remember the people and institutions in my community that did not share my holistic perspective of caring for the personal and social dimensions of all people. There were times when I felt like Nehemiah, who said to the Jewish leaders, "You see the distress that we are in, how Jerusalem lies waste, and its gates are burned with fire. Come and let us build the wall of Jerusalem, that we may no longer be a reproach" (Nehemiah 2:17). But many did not respond to the call.

Often, I found church leaders wanting to emphasize personal conversion at the expense of social responsibility. At other times, I witnessed them making decisions on the basis of non-biblical worldviews — a practice that has birthed and promoted countless personal faiths that are subject to individuals' personalities. I have heard charismatic preaching that reflects little to no theological education or understanding. Not surprisingly, biblical illiteracy is widespread. In many ways, the full counsel of God is not being transmitted to the current and future generations.

As the body of Christ, the church is endowed with the potential to be the most transformative force in the world, through the power and guidance of the Holy Spirit. The church has the benefit of God's message of love, compassion, grace, and redemption. Yet many churches have maintained a separation between the sacred and secular, while others have adopted secular practices and still others have borrowed so many elements from other religions that they have lost their Christian distinctiveness. Society desperately needs the church to address the multitude of social issues and needs in the world. Yet the church has not always acted on its call to be an agent of restoration and reconciliation.

Throughout my ministry, I always have been vocal about my view that the church can do much more than it has done to respond to both personal and social issues in the society. At the same time, I am living proof that speaking for God to your community does not always result in positive responses. Abraham and Lot had conflict, even though Abraham had brought his nephew with him and shared his blessings (Genesis 13:1-13). The Israelites chastised Moses for leading them to their death in the wilderness, even though he had fulfilled his God-given call to bring them out of Egypt (Exodus 4:11-12). Jeremiah was treated as a pessimist, traitor, and cynic, and was even put in jail (Jeremiah 37:11-16). Even Jesus was not received in his own hometown (Luke 4:24).

For this reason, you may have to confront your community, so that it works for its spiritual and social renewal. In fact, God may be calling you to be today's John the Baptist, who confronted his own community during Roman captivity in both the religious and political arenas. As John challenged the Pharisees and Sadducees who held religious power in his day, he also spoke out against King Herod Antipas, the tetrarch of Galilee and Perea during Jesus' life. Herod had married his brother's wife Herodias — an act that was against the Mosaic Law (Leviticus 18:16; 20:21; Mark 6:18). Like John, Herod was Jewish, even though he and his father, King Herod the Great, were both reported to have catered to Roman power and Greek traditions. This rebuke angered Herod and consequently won John incarceration. While John did not seek this outcome, he was faithful to his call to advance kingdom values, so he did not think twice about confronting Herod.

Sure enough, Herodias wanted Herod to kill John the Baptist for his attack. Herod had the secular authority to make this happen, but he knew that Jewish law forbade it. Also, John was a righteous and holy man, so Herod resisted (Mark 6:18-20). Herodias's anger did not fade away, however. At a party in his honor, in the presence of nobles, military commanders, and leading men of Galilee, Herod offered to grant Herodias's daughter, Salome, whatever she asked of him — up to half his kingdom (6:21-23). At Herodias's insistence, Salome asked for "the head of John the Baptist on a platter" (6:24-25). Of course, Herod could have refused this request. But he succumbed to the whims of his illegitimate wife and her daughter and reluctantly beheaded John (6:26-28). In the end, Herod was more beholden to the oath he made with Salome, and to the opinions of others, than he was to being faithful to the Mosaic Law. Alas, social civilities trumped godly justice.

While in his own right John may not have chosen the path that led to his death, he knew his call was part of a greater plan in which God had involved him. He accepted that failure by the people to heed and repent did not release him from his responsibility to confront his own community. John had to inform his community of God's movement in Jesus Christ and the Kingdom of God, for they were God's covenant community. Some listened and repented, and others did not. Either way, he went on "baptizing in the wilderness and proclaiming a baptism of repentance for the forgiveness of sins" (Mark 1:4), until his untimely and brutal death by the political and religious powers.

If you accept God's call to minister in captivity, God's covenant community will certainly listen at some times — and reject the prophetic message at other times. It may even shun you and become openly hostile, which could make your charge seem an insurmountable task. But you must trust that God will be with you. When you confront your community, you can accomplish four things. First, you can ensure that the community acts on its godly mandate. Second, you can oppose the existing status quo. Third, you can move institutions to support the community. Finally, you can involve God in peace and justice efforts. Ultimately, your efforts will be instrumental in realizing the shalom of society.

Ensure That the Community Acts on Its Godly Mandate

Regrettably, the institutional church has not always acted according to its godly mandate. Indeed, the church has not always looked within itself before looking outside. Certainly judgment has not always begun at the house of God (1 Peter 4:17). In fact, the church at times has advanced a message of intolerance and has perpetrated atrocities in the name of Christ: wars, land takeovers, overthrows of foreign governments, slavery, Jim Crow, abusive state-sanctioned labor practices, anti-immigrant laws and practices, mistreatment of the poor and marginalized. The list goes on. In these situations, the church has moved away from its purpose of being the light and salt of the earth.

God called the prophet Ezekiel to confront the covenant community in the midst of Babylonian captivity. First, the Holy Spirit entered Ezekiel and set him on his feet, thus enabling Ezekiel to hear God (2:2). Then, God told Ezekiel to charge the covenant community for not having acted in accordance with its godly mandate — even though God knew the people would not listen to him (Ezekiel 2:3-5). At the same time, God revealed to Ezekiel that his success was not dependent on being favorably received by the people. Instead, it depended only on the acknowledgement by the people that a prophet had been among them (2:5).

God also advised Ezekiel not to be afraid of the people, their words, or even their looks (2:6). His charge was to speak God's words to them, which God had given him directly (2:7-8). Given the rebelliousness of the covenant community, it is not surprising that the message included words of lamentation and mourning and woe (2:10). It also is not startling that Ezekiel felt bitterness about his conceivably fruitless call. Still, we learn that the hand of God was strong upon him, which enabled Ezekiel to be among the captive community despite feeling overwhelmed (3:14-15). As you minister in captivity by confronting your community, you too must let God's hand be strong upon you.

Confronting your community today will often mean addressing the dichotomy or separation between the sacred and the secular, and the personal and the social. The majority of churches focus on either saving souls or changing the world's systems and structures. As we saw in Chapter 3, we even have reduced these approaches to competing categories: personal piety (the individual gospel) versus social justice (the social gospel). Indeed, many who have tried to merge these two perspectives have found tension, fear, resistance, and accusations of proclaiming a "watered-down" or fragmented message. In the process, the church has not embraced a holistic approach to life. This is as if Ezra, Jerusalem's temple priest, was without Nehemiah during the Persian captivity. Or as if Nehemiah, Jerusalem's community developer, was without Ezra. In other words, both are needed.

As you confront your community, you will likely have to serve as a bridge. You may have to steer proponents of a personal gospel beyond the personal dimensions of their faith to incorporate social justice. This will include involving them in community development issues, such as affordable housing, voter registration, police brutality, quality health care, immigration, welfare reform, and school reform. Or, you may have to steer proponents of a social gospel beyond the social dimensions of their faith to incorporate personal piety. This will include helping them to cultivate such practices as individual and corporate prayer, confession, Bible study, fasting, worship, meditation, and reflection.

Remember how John the Baptist was in the wilderness calling people to repent, preparing the way for Christ (Matthew 3:2). At one point, the Pharisees and Sadducees went to see John, claiming they were there for baptism (3:7). As you may know, the Pharisees were the prominent religious party in Judaism, while the Sadducees were the majority of the Sanhedrin — the Jewish court in Jerusalem. Both interpreted the Law of Moses in a way that emphasized personal piety at the expense of justice. Discerning that their motives were impure, John exhorted them to become aligned with the principles of the coming Kingdom of God, and professed the power of Christ, which he concluded was even greater than his as a prophet:

> Therefore bear fruits worthy of repentance, and do not think to say to yourselves, "We have Abraham as our father." For I say to you that God is able to raise up children to Abraham from these stones. And even now the ax is laid to the root of the trees. Therefore every tree which does not bear good fruit is cut down and thrown into the fire. I indeed baptize you with water unto repentance, but he who is coming after me is mightier than I, whose sandals I am not worthy to carry. He will baptize you with the Holy Spirit and fire. His winnowing fan is in his hand, and he will thoroughly clean out his threshing floor, and gather his wheat into the barn; but he will burn up the chaff with unquenchable fire. (Matthew 3:8-12)

John was aware of the power and influence of the Pharisees and Sadducees, but he also understood that the rule of God was more powerful and influential than their one-sided adherence to the Mosaic Law. While the Pharisees and Sadducees wanted to maintain a truncated gospel, Christ was bringing a holistic gospel, which would address the personal *and* social dimensions of the people's lives. John understood that he had been entrusted with creating a path for Christ's message.

THE REFORMED CHURCH IN AMERICA AND THE HISPANIC COUNCIL

John the Baptist's conviction was very much in my mind when I confronted the Reformed Church in America in 1976, while I was the pastor of Melrose Reformed Church.[1] As I became more involved in the denominational life of the RCA, I quickly learned that Melrose was not the only Reformed church having to deal with racial transition in its neighborhood. In fact, this was happening across the region and across the country, which led to many conversations with other Hispanic missions groups within the denomination about the need to organize ourselves into one voice.

I began organizing the pockets of Hispanics in the denomination's New York City and New Jersey congregations. As a result, we established a Hispanic Council, and I was elected its first president. Immediately we began to advocate, coordinate, and serve as the collective voice of Hispanics within the denomination. We also petitioned the national RCA board to fund an Office of National Hispanic Ministries that would work with Hispanics within and outside of the church. The board granted the request, and I became the first Secretary for Hispanic Ministries, a full-time executive position within the denomination. For this role, I left Melrose, which had become predominantly Puerto Rican and Hispanic during my three years there.

As the Secretary for Hispanic Ministries, I worked with churches in the United States and Venezuela, and had an informal relationship with churches in Mexico. In this new position, I traveled to places in the United States that I had never imagined, including Holland, Michigan, and Sioux Center, Iowa. I became very familiar with mainstream America, which I had previously only known through television. Yet in these new surroundings I encountered the same dichotomized gospel, only in different forms. On a visit to Holland, Michigan, for instance, I stayed at an elder's home from one of the larger congregations. After my sermon, he complimented me on being passionate and full of enthusiasm, and remarked on how well the congregation responded to it. Then he complimented me for not being "like the other Mexicans in town." Of course, he did not bother to find out that I was Puerto Rican and not Mexican.

Later on this same visit he took me to Christian-owned migrant camps that were in deplorable condition, and it did not seem to register

1. Again, Justo Gonzalez impacted me in terms of his prophetic role with a dominant-culture denomination, and how the Hispanic community spoke to that reality. In *Mañana: Christian Theology from a Hispanic Perspective* (Nashville: Abingdon Press, 1990), he accurately captured the unique role of the Hispanic community, given that U.S. Hispanics have been both the oppressor and the oppressed throughout their history in the United States and in Latin America.

with him that it was not Christian behavior to run a camp for migrant workers in this way. I began to understand that even though one accepted Jesus Christ in one's personal life, it did not automatically mean that one transcended one's sociopolitical context. Before me was a Christian who professed Jesus Christ as Lord and Savior in his personal life, but who, in social interactions and in his view of other people, blatantly contradicted what he professed. He simply did not consider the ethical implications of his faith in his daily life.

I began to see this as a recurring theme in my ministry. The gospel, as it was being proclaimed and practiced, was being truncated, divided, compartmentalized, and fragmented. It was responding to issues of personal transformation. It dealt with parts of individuals' lives, but not the totality. It did not engage or confront the social reality in which people lived outside the four walls of the church. This kind of gospel made it easy for a person to be a devout, pious worshiper on Sunday, and — to put it bluntly — a bigoted racist from Monday to Saturday. It was possible to be a spiritual authority on Sunday, even be an office holder in the church, and be an exploiter and oppressor of people the rest of the week.

There seemed to be an emerging, clear, and unbroken thread from El Camino, Melrose, and now the RCA national church community. And it was something I just could not accept. I was persuaded that the gospel's calling was to submit our *whole* lives to the rule and authority of God. I decided that the Hispanic Council which I was already leading would adopt and advocate a holistic ministry approach within individual churches and in the denomination. As a result the council and its work became hard to categorize; we did not fit on one side or the other of the traditional personal piety/social gospel divide. We also began to attract controversy.

The Hispanic Council members were highly evangelistic, focusing on fasting, praying, piety, and the charismatic gifts. We held spiritual retreats. We recruited Hispanic students into denominational seminaries and Hispanic ministers into the denomination. We secured the first Hispanic professor at New Brunswick Theological Seminary, one of the denomination's two schools for ministers. We established a formal relationship with the Pentecostal Union of Churches in Venezuela. We emphasized church growth, planting churches throughout the country that were growing significantly, including congregations in Brooklyn and Rochester, New York; Chicago; Los Angeles; Denver; various locations in Florida; and Holland and Grand Rapids, Michigan.

At the same time, we were highly political, confronting systems and structures and addressing social issues such as racism, sexism, and colonialism. Toward this end, we forged coalitions with the other minority councils within the denomination. With our growing influence, we successfully submitted resolutions for systemic change to the general assembly of the denomination. We called for denominational resolutions seeking divestment and an end to apartheid in South Africa; freedom for several Puerto Rican political prisoners who had been in jail for over a quarter-century; humanitarian aid for the pro-independence forces in Rhodesia (modern-day Zimbabwe); and support for a national boycott against lettuce in support of Cesar Chavez and his migrant workers movement. We were Hispanics, blacks, Asians, and Native Americans making sure the denomination acted on its godly mandate. To us, Christ was on our side.

Oppose the Status Quo Maintained by Your Community

My experience at the RCA and in other ministries reinforced my belief that many churches have embraced non-Christian values and perpetuated a self-righteousness that allows other influences to distort their godly message. I have seen many Christians embrace excessive consumerism (material prosperity) as the optimal expression of God's blessing, rather than seek the contentment that Paul sought for himself and others.

> Not that I speak in regard to need, for I have learned in whatever state I am, to be content: I know how to be abased, and I know how to abound. Everywhere and in all things I have learned both to be full and to be hungry, both to abound and to suffer need. (Philippians 4:11-12)

They have not heeded the writer of Hebrews, who warned us about financial prosperity.

> Keep your life free from love of money, and be content with what you have, for he has said, "I will never leave you nor forsake you." (Hebrews 13:5)

Others have embraced a kind of nebulous otherworldliness. Still others have combined Christianity with nationalism or patriotism, holding the belief that security is achieved solely through military strength, rather than through standing up for peace and justice for all people. In all these cases, the gospel is distorted, and its holistic message is obscured.

In many churches, religious elites have become entrenched and self-perpetuating. They benefit from their participation in institutionalized poverty and oppression. Their worship services have great sacramental and liturgical beauty, but their churches have veered from addressing community needs. In such cases, the church preserves the reign of the powers. It also diminishes its influence and leadership to denounce and call the powers, and their systems and structures, to accountability. Such congregations are clearly recognized by society as lacking in moral authority, and Jesus announces that he will confront these churches for being spiritually lukewarm:

> So then, because you are lukewarm, and neither cold nor hot, I will vomit you out of my mouth. For you say, "I am rich, have become wealthy, and have need of nothing" — and do not know that you are wretched, miserable, poor, blind, and naked. (Revelation 3:16-17)

Comfortableness with the status quo is not confined to one side of the church or the other; over the years, I have confronted it in the side that demonizes community and political work, as well as in the side that demonizes reliance on God to bring about community development. At times, members and leaders of both sides have resisted my call to reform. When churches have evangelism and crusades as their primary focus, I have applauded them for proclaiming the gospel, but I have pointed out that good works have not always followed their faith. They may be concerned with the afterlife, or at best with individual Christians accessing an abundant quality of life in this present time, but they neglect the issues of collective sin and social responsibility, and are falling short of going beyond the personal. They do not deal with reform issues, including social justice. I remind them that this view is a spiritualized version of American rugged individualism. It is a "me" gospel, which does not respond to the community or to the public dimensions of their faith.

When churches have community and political work as their primary focus, I have applauded them for the good works their faith has inspired, but have pointed out that they have not always proclaimed the spiritual dimension of the gospel. They may be concerned with systemic reform and change, or, at best, with people accessing material resources for daily living, but they are neglecting the issues of personal sin and individual responsibility, and are falling short of going beyond the social. They do not deal with afterlife issues, including eternal salvation. I remind them that this view is a spiritualized version of Marxism. It is a "we" gospel, which does not respond to the personal or the individual dimensions of our faith.

I remember that while the Bronx was burning in the 1970s, the churches were burning with Holy Ghost fire inside. Yet so many congregation members accepted that as long as their temples were unscathed, they did not have to deal with the challenges besetting the surrounding community. Some even believed that the people had brought their plight upon themselves — a punishment from God and not the result of cruelty perpetrated by opportunists who were seeking to profit from insurance claims and other government benefits. Churches missed the opportunity to be light and salt in that community, choosing to focus on private prayer and fasting and failing to lead the way to God-centered community development.[2]

Yet those churches that did take a stand for social justice often were too willing to overlook personal failings. At times, church and community leaders became so preoccupied with working for social change that they turned a deaf ear to ethical failings of individuals. They found it easier to confront the powers than to challenge those who they feared would hurt their chances to achieve the desired change. Instances of infidelity, substance abuse, and other immoral personal behaviors were sidestepped as long as people were loyal to the cause. The leaders who sidestepped them also missed the opportunity to be light and salt in the community, choosing to focus on their public agenda and not leading the way to godly, holistic living, service, and leadership.

ASSEMBLY OF CHRISTIAN CHURCHES/ YOUTH EVANGELISM

One of my earliest memories of opposing the status quo is of an experience that happened when I was an eighteen-year-old exhorter in the Assembly of Christian Churches. Several members of my church youth

---

2. At the same time, there have been glimpses of holistic ministry within the Pentecostal church, including the Damascus Youth Crusade, Way Out, and Teen Challenge. Also, the Pentecostal church's focus on reading the Scriptures became one of the largest (albeit unintentional) literacy programs for adult learners.

group and I founded an organization we called Youth Evangelism (YE); our guiding biblical text was Mark 16:15: "And he said unto them, Go ye into all the world, and preach the gospel to every creature" (KJV). We saw the word "ye" in that verse as an abbreviation for Youth Evangelism.

On the surface, this might not seem like an act of challenging the status quo. But our actions were in fact unprecedented. The Assembly already had a youth association and a missions department. But we wanted our own institution. We believed in youth empowerment, and decision-making seemed distant in the hands of the Assembly. As an organization, we raised our own funds and sent a team of youth to Guatemala for several months. We supported the team directly and not through the denomination's mission department. The denomination became angry because we did not use traditional youth and missions channels and we included youth from other denominations and conferences in the charter. Yet the Assembly allowed its adult members to join other fellowships as long as those entities did not have ordination power; we felt that the same privileges should be granted to us, so that we could engage in ministry and missions.

At the annual convention, the adult leaders called us to arbitration and ordered us to rescind YE, resign from it as individuals, or submit it to the Assembly's control. We challenged them on several principles. First, we pointed out that YE was a membership organization, and we wanted to fellowship with other parts of the body of Christ. Second, we insisted that YE had its own mission, which was to empower young people to enter the mission field. Third, YE was raising its own funds, so we deserved to make our own decisions instead of having them handed down by the missions department. Finally, we did not believe we were violating any of the Assembly's laws or regulations. The leadership held committee meetings over two days, seeking ways to humble us. But we refused to submit, and in the end no resolution was reached. Regrettably, many of the young ministers in YE, including evangelist Manny Rosa and Rev. Hector Seda, subsequently left the denomination — but not without having made a strong effort to challenge the status quo.

Move Institutions to Support the Community

That early experience with Youth Evangelism was a fight for my own Christian institution, one that I cared about and felt closely connected to.

Yet it was also an effort to move a larger Christian institution — the Assembly — to address the needs of its constituents. The church as an organization has not always supported the larger community; it has even been part of the system of oppression. The church has not always been a serving institution that supports its immediate community; instead, at times it has been insensitive, co-opting, and controlling, with little regard to the interests of the larger community, unless it served its purpose.

When different parts of the body of Christ embrace holistic ministry, they are challenged with the idea of sharing power and resources with other people and institutions. Yet too often, they fail to relate to others, let alone truly share power and resources. In these situations many churches want to take advantage of the material and political benefits of alliances with others, and also to present an appearance of diversity.[3] Yet they also want to have a monopoly on the administrative gifts of the body. They want decision-making power to remain in the hands of an inner circle of institutional guardians. When this is the case, it takes a concerted effort of confrontation to alter the power dynamics and release the available resources to the larger population.

In fact, this was the case with the early Christian church. Even though Christ had given the church a clear commission to bring the gospel to the entire world (Matthew 28:18-20), the church initially stayed in Jerusalem and its established leaders connected its ministry to Jewish identity and the historical process of Judaism. For the most part, it retained the notion of a restored kingdom of Israel, only now to be led by Jesus, whom it expected to return shortly. The church's members had not grasped the fullness of the revelation they received, that the message was for the whole world. They were not called to restore the Davidic kingdom. Instead, they were entrusted with proclaiming the evangel, Jesus Christ, to the whole world.

But after the Holy Spirit empowered it to carry out its ministry at Pentecost (Acts 2:1-4), the church began to truly serve the needs of the community, providing to each individual member according to his or her need, and utilizing its own resources to serve the needs of the broader

---

3. Here, I was influenced by Paulo Freire and Frantz Fanon (from a race perspective), who spoke of the danger of the oppressed becoming the oppressor, as well as the oppressor becoming our role model. Thus, when the oppressed experience liberation and attain power, they have the potential to employ that oppressive model. In particular, I was impacted by Freire's *Pedagogy of the Oppressed* (New York: Herder and Herder, 1970) and Fanon's *The Wretched of the Earth* (New York: Grove Press, 1965).

community (Acts 2:42-47). It began to identify people in the community to serve the larger community and ensure that all the poor and needy were being served with no prejudice (6:1-7). *What people needed,* not who they were, became its criterion for ministry. Of course, in these early days the church still consisted mainly of Jewish Christians, but it was beginning to include more and more gentiles. In fact, it was the result of the Greek Christians confronting the status quo concerning the daily distribution that the Jewish Christian leaders identified a core group of Greek Christians. Thereafter, the church provided for all its members.

In the face of persecution, the church also was learning that it could not be exclusive. So it adopted and implemented new strategies of word and deed to fulfill Christ's mandate for all humankind. So Stephen preached his first sermon in Judea (Acts 7), and Philip went down to Samaria (8:5). This message eventually reached Antioch and continued to the far reaches of the Roman Empire. Thus, the church broadened its scope to include converting gentiles and even agents of the oppressive empire, including Cornelius and his household (Acts 10).

Of course, as the church grew more established and more powerful it once again became comfortable operating from and within its traditions, often failing to recognize and validate new opportunities. It has sometimes missed God's time and purpose and advances in his Kingdom-agenda. The church has sometimes seen me as a rabble-rouser who was challenging its methodology of service and questioning its approaches; instead, it could have embraced me as part of God's ongoing movement, helping them to be better equipped to carry out the next stage of their mission, including embracing and serving new populations and constituencies. Nevertheless, I was not about to let the church's resistance stop me from carrying out my ministry call.

Lutheran Medical Center

In 1971, I became the community coordinator for pastoral care at the Lutheran Medical Center, which was my first experience working in an institutional setting. I ministered to patients at the hospital and served as the liaison to the surrounding Hispanic and other urban congregations. Here again I came face-to-face with Puerto Rican pastors being marginalized. They did not have the same access or respect that Anglo pastors were given. They were considered nonprofessionals. When I inquired, hospital officials said the Puerto Rican clergy lacked seminary training or courses in clinical pastoral education. I reminded the institution that these were bona fide pastors with churches incorporated in New York City, and under the law they had the same rights as any other pastor. They responded that there were certain institutional dynamics of ministry in the hospital that these pastors were not familiar with, and that they could only learn them in a clinical pastoral education, or CPE, course.

When I investigated further, I found out that pastors had to be seminary graduates or had to be attending seminary to take the CPE course — something that simply wasn't emphasized in the Puerto Rican church culture. I did not accept this as the final word and began to challenge the institution to equip these clergy, who served a majority of its patients. Instinctively, I became an advocate of this underserved community. I realized that I was uniquely positioned to speak for this voiceless population. Indeed, a hospital, even a Christian hospital, could represent the worldly powers. Thus, I met with hospital officials and demanded parity, respect, and the same access for these people.

Ultimately, the hospital conceded to these demands. I began working with indigenous pastors and recruited six of them, promising them scholarships to enroll in a course that dealt with the institutional dynamics of ministering in hospitals. They agreed and took this course with an accredited CPE supervisor. This process had to be approved by the national Association of Clinical Pastoral Education, by the local board of trustees of the hospital, and by the pastoral care department. The local congregations also had to give their pastors permission to enter this program.

I convinced the pastors that it would be an enriching experience, so their churches agreed. This allowed me to develop a CPE training program for Puerto Rican pastors, designed to fill the institutional gap between the culture of the hospital, the culture of ministry in the hospital, and the culture of the indigenous churches. I served as a course assistant to the CPE supervisor, helping to give seminars that were informative, interactive, and dealt with health issues, faith issues, and issues related to the individual and group counseling they experienced as part of the CPE process.

As the Puerto Rican pastors became more fully integrated into the life of the hospital, the institution learned to deal with the indigenous clergy, and also the indigenous clergy learned how to minister within an institutional setting. The program was a success. Every pastor graduated, and two of the six in that first class, Rev. Milton Donato and Rev. Tony Garcia, became institutional hospital chaplains. They went on to do several more quarters of CPE and then two-year residencies after which they became bona fide institutional chaplains of hospitals in the field. Subsequently, the program opened the door for Latino clergy to become institutional chaplains in hospitals and prisons throughout the city. It became a model.

NEW YORK THEOLOGICAL SEMINARY

In 1973, as I was completing my tenure at the Lutheran Medical Center and beginning my pastorate at the Melrose Reformed Church, I learned about the New York Theological Seminary (NYTS) through several Anglo students in the Lutheran Medical Center's pastoral care department. I subsequently met with the school's president, Rev. Dr. William Webber,[4]

---

4. After I met Dr. Webber, I read his books and was struck by how much spiritual insight I received from someone whom my wing of the church considered a religious liberal. The more I read, the more I found the Bible to be at the center of his writings. Also, the context was inner city urban communities in the United States. He resonated with the issues that I was dealing with experientially on a daily basis: racism, ethnocentrism, sexism, war, and poverty. He also was dealing with them from a biblical perspective. The books that most impacted me were *God's Colony in Man's World* (Nashville: Abingdon Press, 1960); *The Congregation in Mission: Emerging Structures for the Church in an Urban Society* (Nashville: Abingdon Press, 1964); and, later, *Today's Church: A Community of Exiles and Pilgrims* (Nashville: Abingdon Press, 1979).

At the same time, I lived with tension with Dr. Webber. He was the founder of the East Harlem Protestant Parish (EHPP), which was perceived and hailed in mainline Protestant circles in the U.S. as the model for the Protestant church ministering in inner city communities. It also was very prominent in urban theological literature and theologies. On the other hand, the Puerto Rican community saw EHPP and its heirs as oppressors. This was further reinforced by the doctoral thesis of Rev. Dr. Benjamin Alicea-Lugo, which was a comprehensive study of how EHPP was a model of colonial leadership in East Harlem. Not surprisingly, Dr. Alicea-Lugo was criticized in mainline Protestant circles for suggesting that a respected theologian like Dr. Webber would perpetuate such a model.

When I worked in East Harlem for the local assemblyman, Angelo Del Toro, I connected to indigenous Puerto Rican organizations in East Harlem. In my interactions, I learned that they perceived the EHPP model as a white paternalistic, condescending, colonial leadership model that aimed to save their "brown heathen brothers." In sharp contrast, the EHPP model was accepted by the African American community and actually developed partnerships with them. The Puerto Rican leadership saw this relationship as being motivated by white guilt. They also believed that the white Protestant leadership was pro–African American at the expense of East Harlem's Puerto Rican leadership.

As an active church minister and Puerto Rican leader in East Harlem, I was caught in to express my desire to attend NYTS and reconcile the duality I had been experiencing concerning the sacred and secular. He explained to me that I could not study there because I did not have a bachelor's degree.

I challenged the school's policy on the grounds that Pentecostal churches were growing without pastors having bachelor's degrees, while mainline churches were not growing even though their pastors had bachelor's degrees. I argued that the role of a seminary was to prepare pastors for ministry irrespective of whether they had a college education. In response, he challenged me to identify thirty to forty indigenous Pentecostal pastors who were interested in enrolling in a college program at the seminary for established pastors.

After a few months, I came back to Dr. Webber with the names of these pastors, and he sought and received funding from the Lilly Endowment to establish the program in conjunction with Adelphi University. This program was the first of its kind in the country and served as the prototype of seminary-undergraduate partnerships throughout the country and other parts of the world. An offshoot of this encounter was that NYTS named a Hispanic dean, Dr. Esdras Betancourt, and became a magnet for Puerto Rican clergy. Already, it was attracting African American clergy. And I became a trustee of the seminary, which enabled me to impact it beyond these initiatives.

Involve God in Peace and Justice Efforts

Very early on in my ministry, I learned that Christians were not the only ones confronting the powers around Kingdom-related issues. In Matthew 25:31-46, Jesus' parable illustrates the point of unconsciously "working for

---

that tension. At some level, the white Protestant leadership, including Dr. Webber, saw itself as fostering a biblical progressive agenda, rooted in transcendence and multicultural leadership, with which I resonated. At the same time, I saw my own Puerto Rican community in East Harlem where I was born being oppressed by both white and African American leaders. Here I was working within the Puerto Rican community to advance a nationalistic, community-controlled agenda. At the same time, I felt slightly uncomfortable because I knew that, in the end, we would have to unite and reconcile with African Americans and not fight over the crumbs that the system was distributing. In other words, I was part of the Jerusalem church, even though I understood that I needed to move toward the Antioch church and the liberation of all oppressed people. But Puerto Ricans were lowest on the totem pole, and we just wanted a piece of the pie.

the Kingdom." Those who were on the right of the king asked him where he was when they served the needy. His response? "Inasmuch as you did it to one of the least of these my brethren, you did it to me" (25:40). They were serving God without knowing. To God, doing ministry to the "least of these" is directly serving him. In some way, and it is a mystery, he incarnates himself in the suffering of the people.

This passage of Scripture led me to connect with those community groups that I discerned were directly serving people without a full understanding that they were serving the King himself. Thus, I began to network with people and institutions around peace and justice issues. In the process, I brought Christian prayer and other spiritual disciplines, to bring a witness for the peace and justice that Christ brings and seeks for everyone. In most cases, they received this because of our relationships and our mutual accountability.

By being in their midst, I authenticated my witness. I gained a hearing. If I had refused to leave the confines of my group, I would not have had a voice or ever provided an opportunity for those outside the community to meet the living God. I think about Daniel and the three Hebrew youths, who were in the Babylonian king's court alongside those who practiced other religions and worshiped other gods. This did not stop Daniel or the young men from having a presence there, or from interpreting visions and dreams (Daniel 2:31-45). Indeed, their perseverance in maintaining their beliefs led to King Nebuchadnezzar and later Persian King Darius to declare the superiority of the God of Daniel and the three Hebrew youths (4:1-3; 6:25-28).

I also reflect on the Apostle Paul, who followed a similar incarnational approach. At the Areopagus or Mars Hill — a traditional meeting space in Athens — Paul brought light and revelation to those in attendance by using the established understanding of the supernatural to reveal Christ to them: "For as I was passing through and considering the objects of your worship, I even found an altar with this inscription: 'To the unknown god.' Therefore, the One whom you worship without knowing, him I proclaim to you" (Acts 17:22-23). Paul did not dismantle or deconstruct their prevailing spiritual framework. Instead, he affirmed the common ground they shared and then went on to describe the particular manifestation of this universal perspective, which for him culminated in Jesus Christ. He ended up achieving conversion from some of the hearers by being faithful to his responsibility to proclaim the gospel in non-Christian and nontraditional spaces.

Thus, with issues like police brutality and racial profiling, and the cases of Anthony Baez and Amadou Diallo, I struggled alongside the New Black Panther Party, the Latin Kings, Maoists, the Communist Party, the Socialist Party, and many other groups. Around education reform, I worked with the teachers' union and local community and organizing groups. Around immigration reform, I worked with Make the Road New York, the Hispanic Federation, the New York Immigration Coalition, and the Latino Leadership Circle (also a Christian group). I also became active in an interfaith sanctuary movement that provided refuge for undocumented immigrants who received deportation letters.

Along the way, I have connected people and institutions to promoters of holistic ministry within their tradition. To the social justice churches and non-Christian grassroots organizing groups, I have pointed to Cesar Chavez marching with the Virgen de Guadalupe. I reminded people that Rev. Dr. Martin Luther King Jr. and the Southern Christian Leadership Conference prayed and invoked the name of the Lord. Mother Teresa and her order of nuns cared for the impoverished. Mama Leo (Rev. Leoncia Rosado) cared for the drug-addicted. To non-Christians, I have mentioned Gandhi and Malcolm X fighting for peace and justice. These individuals were unapologetic about a spiritual dimension being an integral part of their community work.

In personal piety churches, I pointed to biblical figures (Nehemiah, Isaiah, Paul) as well as contemporary figures (Mama Leo, John Perkins) who interacted with the world from the perspective of their Kingdom values. I showed them how these and other individuals were unapologetic about community work being an integral part of their spiritual dimension. They also were unapologetic about their community convictions being an integral part of their spiritual work. They understood that spiritual activity was integral to their ministry.

In the process, I was able to bring the message of captivity theology and holistic ministry. Regardless of who was involved, I found that people were more open to views that were outside their theological or philosophical constructs when they saw me struggling alongside them. Indeed, being incarnational mattered! This was the case when it comes to my involvement with the Young Lords Party and the People's Church.[5]

---

5. The Young Lords Party represented in my psyche Puerto Rican manhood in the urban context. They, as naïve as it may have been, struck back at what they perceived was part of the system of oppression: the First Spanish Methodist Church. They also connected

YOUNG LORDS PARTY
AND THE PEOPLE'S CHURCH

It was 1969, and the Black Panthers, Brown Berets, Students for a Democratic Society, and the Yippies were making headlines across the country. In Chicago and New York, the Young Lords Party, a Puerto Rican gang turned revolutionary political party, was raising all kinds of controversy and turmoil. That summer, they took over the First Spanish Methodist Church in East Harlem and evicted the congregation from its building. They claimed that the church was not serving the community and that their takeover was what "true Christianity" was all about.

I was a young minister in 1969, and I was moved to go to the People's Church (as they had renamed First Spanish Methodist) to see what all the uproar was about. To my surprise, when I entered the church, other ministers were already there. They were leaders within the Christian community. The police were about to remove the Young Lords by physical force, so we quickly formed a ministers' group to try to mediate the situation.

As I stared across the meeting room, I noticed my childhood friend, Felipe Luciano. He was now chairman of the Young Lords Party. It was one of those unexplainable, unexpected moments. There we were, two childhood friends, who had grown up in the same church. I had become a minister and he a political revolutionary.[6] The good thing was that we

---

urban Puerto Ricans to the larger struggle for Puerto Rican independence on the island, as well as Latin American and Caribbean independence and anti-colonial struggles. For more on the history of the Young Lords, you can view the documentary *Palante, Siempre Palante! The Young Lords* (New York: Third World Newsreel, 1996), produced by Young Lord Iris Morales. Also, see Juan González's *Harvest of Empire: A History of Latinos in America* (New York: Penguin Books, 2001), and Miguel "Mickey" Melendez's *We Took the Streets: Fighting for Latino Rights with the Young Lords* (Piscataway, NJ: Rutgers University Press, 2003).

6. I was fond of Felipe and others who took back their history and identity, and emphasized their contextual reality. This included Claude Brown, Eldridge Cleaver, Alex Haley, Dick Gregory, and Piri Thomas. These individuals appropriated role models and status symbols from their own history, which helped me do the same from my context of the Puerto Rican Pentecostal community. I was impacted by several of their writings, including the following: Claude Brown, *Manchild in the Promised Land* (New York: Penguin Group, 1966); Eldridge Cleaver, *Soul on Ice* (New York: McGraw Hill, 1968); Alex Haley, *Autobiography of Malcolm X* (New York: Random House, 1976); Dick Gregory with Robert Lipsyte, *Nigger: An Autobiography* (New York: E. P. Dutton, 1964); Piri Thomas, *Down These Mean Streets* (New York: Signet Books, 1968); and *Savior, Savior, Hold My Hand* (New York: Knopf Doubleday Publishing Group, 1972).

trusted one another, and in some ways, we always tried to support each other. For this reason, my organization, Youth Evangelism, held a press conference and supported the services that the Young Lords were providing out of the People's Church, which included a breakfast program, x-rays, and other services.

At the same time, several anti-poverty community organizations were holding demonstrations across the city for an increase in services to the Puerto Rican community. The Young Lords denounced these organizations and their leaders as "poverty pimps." But they were willing to speak to me to try to keep communications open in our community between these two factions. In the process, I served as a bridge builder and reconciler. I also got to share my faith in Jesus Christ as Lord and Savior, who, I reminded them, could bring peace and justice to the society.

THE ZEN PEACEMAKER ORDER AND THE BEARING WITNESS RETREAT

Several decades later, I participated in the annual Bearing Witness Retreat of Bernie Glassman's Zen Peacemaker Order at the invitation of Francisco "Paco" Lugovina, an ordained Buddhist priest and a friend of over forty years. This interfaith event remembers and bears witness to the Holocaust and its atrocities at the concentration camps at Auschwitz-Birkenau in Poland. It was the first time a Puerto Rican Pentecostal had spoken at this gathering. I actually preached right in front of the ovens where the bodies of thousands of innocent Jewish people had been burned. I spoke on the theme from Ezekiel, the valley of dry bones, and raised the question, "Will these bones rise again?" In the process, I represented and lifted up the name of Christ.

As I confronted my community, I have dealt with varying challenges that threatened to hurt me and the institutions I ran. But I knew the Lord was behind me. I felt peace and joy when I spoke on behalf of God to the church and the community at large. I did not back down and significant changes occurred; thankfully, church leaders and members responded favorably to many of my requests. I felt the Holy Spirit in the midst, softening their hearts. I hope my efforts help you envision ways that God may be calling you to confront your community.

CHAPTER 6

You Can Engage the Powers!

$\sim$

O ne of the reasons I have been a controversial figure over the course of my ministry has been my willingness to engage non-Christians and non-Christian institutions — what the Christian community has often called "the powers." The times my community has criticized and rejected me the most has been when I engaged the powers and their systems and structures. Some would remind me of Jesus' prayer: "They are not of the world, just as I am not of the world" (John 17:16). Thus, they inferred, I had no business getting involved with the powers. But then I would remind them of the verse that leads up to this statement: "I do not ask that you take them out of the world, but that you keep them from the evil one" (17:15). Jesus does not call us to blind detachment, but to discerning engagement, which requires loyalty to the Kingdom of God and not the kingdom of man (Mark 12:35-40).

By remembering this, I have been able to articulate my Kingdom-minded vision and mission, while not having to compromise my integrity or the outcomes I sought. I was clear that some system agents were aligned with me on peace and justice issues but had different positions on issues such as abortion and same-sex marriage. Others identified with me on the moral agenda but were not with me on political empowerment or social justice issues. Either way, the measuring stick for my engagement was the advancement of Kingdom values. Of course, as fallen entities, the powers sought to garner my loyalty, and even to co-opt me at times. But in those instances, I rejected their non-negotiable deal-breakers. And while they retaliated at times, I have always recalled the many positive results I had when I engaged the powers and have continued my ministry in this arena.

Indeed, the church has engaged the powers many times over the course of its history, both on an individual and a collective level, and has been able to influence the powers to act in accordance with Kingdom values. When societies have experienced reform, revival, or revolution, God's people have in many cases stood alongside the powers, either in a teaching mode or by setting the example. In the process, they have yielded victories around peace and justice issues. They have brought about reconciliation and unity. They have also been able to access resources that otherwise would not have been available to them.

Yet also over the course of the church's history, some Christians have chosen to maintain an attitude of moral and spiritual superiority and rectitude toward the powers. Today, the evangelical wing of the church traditionally has a record of not engaging the powers on peace and justice issues, such as housing for the poor, a livable wage, quality education in the inner cities, and so on. Instead, it has adopted an escapist, otherworldly theology. To the adherents of such a theology, the powers and their systems and structures are intrinsically evil, and the biblical mandate is to be separated from them. "Come out from among them and be separate, says the Lord. Do not touch what is unclean, and I will receive you" (2 Corinthians 6:17). Based on their understanding of such passages as this, they believe that any relationship with the powers would be blasphemous.

They add that God's people are separate from the world, and we cannot mix religion with politics, or work with secular institutions. The idea that God could use unchurched, worldly people in his plan is treated with skepticism or completely dismissed. Instead, the thinking goes, the church should be concerned only about souls. If God had called the church to do something about the society, he would have provided the resources himself. He is sufficient; we do not need anybody or anything else. If we ever did need resources, they surely would come from within the spiritual community. The church should be an *alternative* to secular culture, these Christians believe — or it should even be working to bring down that secular culture![1]

---

1. H. Richard Niebuhr addressed this point in his influential *Christ and Culture* (New York: Harper, 1956). More recently, Stanley Hauerwas addressed this point among evangelicals in his book *The Peaceable Kingdom: A Primer in Christian Ethics* (Notre Dame, IN: University of Notre Dame Press, 1991).

Unfortunately, non-engagement leaves the powers unrestrained. When the church retreats, it abdicates its role to be that shining light on the hill and the salt that preserves the goodness in the society (Matthew 5:13-16). Then, the powers are able to satisfy their institutional self-reliance and indulgences, which has led to corruption, perversions, and oppression. Meanwhile, the church's well-intentioned retreat amounts to nothing more than a rubber stamp for the status quo, and turning into just a social club for its members. It effectively waives its right to be a catalyst for change in the midst of challenging circumstances.

At the same time, engaging the powers does not mean assimilating into the mainstream culture or relinquishing a prophetic role in society. There have been times when the powers have co-opted elements of the Kingdom message, which has made it seem as if they were carrying out a Kingdom agenda. Consequently, many Christians have stood by the powers' reinterpretation of the Kingdom message, and even have become advocates of the powers' non-Kingdom agenda. This has made it more difficult for those who struggle to bring a holistic gospel message of peace and justice. It also has made it easier for the powers to enact unresponsive public policies.

Given that neither retreating from nor assimilating into mainstream culture will do, God may be calling you to be today's Nehemiah. During the Persian captivity, Nehemiah learned about the plight of his people in Jerusalem, who had been left behind after the majority of the people were carried off into exile. They were living in great poverty and distress, and Nehemiah wept and mourned for days (Nehemiah 1:4). He then confessed the role of his people in the community reality and added his household as being partly responsible for their situation (1:5-6). This conviction led Nehemiah to arrive at a community development strategy, for which he engaged the powers to support his efforts. "If it pleases the king, and if your servant has found favor in your sight, I ask that you send me to Judah, to the city of my fathers' tombs, that I may rebuild it" (2:5).

Nehemiah's compassion toward his community, coupled with the self-interest of the powers to keep peace in socio-economically depressed communities, contributed to the favorable response by the system agent:

Furthermore I said to the king, "If it pleases the king, let letters be given to me for the governors of the region beyond the River, that they must permit me to pass through till I come to Judah, and a letter to Asaph the keeper of the king's forest, that he must give me timber to make beams for the gates of the citadel which pertains to the temple, for the city wall, and for the house that I will occupy." And the king granted them to me according to the good hand of my God upon me. (2:7-8)

Thereafter, Nehemiah was able to rally the community to bring about peace and justice.

This is why engaging the powers is beneficial. While you will probably not achieve complete restoration of your society, you can ensure that the powers respond to the needs of its citizens, particularly the most needy. Thus, you can advance Kingdom values to achieve peace and justice. You can be light and salt when engaging systems and structures. You can secure support to advance community initiatives. In the process, you also can manage internal and external tensions in dealing with the powers. Ultimately, people will be able to reside and minister in improved conditions because of your willingness to engage the powers.

Advance Kingdom Values to Achieve Peace and Justice

Historically, the body of Christ has built and cultivated relationships with the powers and has partnered with them on a variety of peace and justice issues. At times, this has enhanced and enriched the powers, and even facilitated peace and justice movements that have transformed the society. A close look at the abolitionist, women's suffrage, civil rights, and labor movements, as well as the contemporary immigration movement, shows how the church has been instrumental in the establishment of these peace and justice policies. In these instances, the church has raised its voice, embracing its prophetic role to advance Kingdom values. In these instances, the church was a prayer on the altar that realized Jesus' supplication, "thy Kingdom come" (Matthew 6:10).

We see the fruit of engagement in the enactment of progressive, sometimes even radical legislation which has benefited the weak, vulnerable, and poor. This legislation has helped the prisoner, the immigrant, the stranger, and the widow and orphan (Matthew 25:31-46). In its intent, it has provided a safety net that at least addresses some of the needs of the marginalized and oppressed. In the process of developing and enacting these new policies, the church has discerned when it could serve as a catalyst for the powers to be agents of personal and social transformation.

Thus, some good has come out of engaging the powers. What the church needs is to discern when it should go in that direction.

In the Scriptures, we see the Persian King Ahasuerus allowing Mordecai, a Jew in exile, to direct public policy that directly affected his community (Esther 8:8-9). This new policy, which gave the Jews the right to defend themselves against those who would harm them, carried the authority and legitimacy of the powers and had far-reaching impact. Mordecai ensured the dissemination of the policy and that the community received and understood it (8:10). In the process, Mordecai gained power and notoriety, which led to many agents of the system helping the covenant community (9:3, 4). Through the efforts of Mordecai, Queen Esther, and others, the covenant community ensured that the powers acted on behalf of peace and justice, which culminated in the community becoming integral parts of the society (9:29–10:3).

U.S. CONGRESSMAN HERMAN BADILLO

I can remember several instances in my own ministry when I advanced Kingdom values and moved system agents to join me in peace and justice efforts. In Chapter 4, I mentioned the rally I organized at the Board of Estimate in support of the rights of New York City's Puerto Rican community. While on one level this is an example of how you can engage your community — the Puerto Rican Pentecostal churches at the time had never before gotten involved in peace and justice efforts — it is also an example of how it is possible to engage the powers productively. In the late 1960s, the Puerto Rican community was not receiving its correct proportion of funds from the city. So I participated in demonstrations and pickets, including a rally at the NYC Board of Estimate, in which many religious leaders, including me, were arrested. Herman Badillo, the former Bronx borough president and U.S. representative, who was a lawyer, agreed to represent us.

I was surprised at how receptive Badillo was to our cause. At the same time, some members of our group objected to his involvement because they disagreed with the policies he enforced when he was commissioner of the NYC Department of Relocation. Many believed that these policies had led to gentrification of some parts of the community. I understood their point of view, but I reminded them that he was one of our highest ranking officials and that his support could be extremely beneficial to us.

So when the leadership got arrested, he represented us. In the end, Badillo became very close to our community and used his legal skills to help us access the powers. Later on, I used his influence to benefit the Puerto Rican community. In later years, he would be one of our community's top spokespersons, even drafting the Congressional act that brought about bilingual education.

NEW YORK STATE SENATOR REV. RUBÉN DÍAZ

In the late 2000s, I engaged New York State Senator Rev. Rubén Díaz on the issue of immigration. Many church pews in the United States today are being filled by immigrants, primarily from Latin America, Africa, and Asia, and these men and women are a vibrant part of the diverse body of Christ. Díaz and his local faith-based organization, the New York Hispanic Clergy Organization, joined the group of indigenous Pentecostal evangelicals that organized an immigration rally in front of 26 Federal Plaza in lower Manhattan. I remember asking Senator Díaz whether the community would come out for an issue that did not deal with same-sex marriage or abortion, both of which the Pentecostal evangelical community was vocal in opposing. He believed we could pull it off, and began to support the planning efforts, having agreed that the time had come for the Pentecostal evangelical community to stand up for their church membership and community residents.

Toward this end, Senator Díaz called Pentecostal bishops to get their support. He also called our local Christian radio stations, and contacted the newspaper *El Diario*. He visited religious councils and their respective constituencies. He also visited the local council of ministers and the ministerial associations. He assured them that they would not be breaking the law by participating in the rally. On the day of the rally, Senator Díaz and his son, Rubén Díaz Jr. (now the Bronx borough president), led the charge to march across the Brooklyn Bridge to 26 Federal Plaza. Indeed, the rally was a success, with some media outlets estimating the crowd at 100,000. I interpreted for Senator Díaz on the stage from Spanish to English during the rally.

U.S. CONGRESSMAN LUIS GUTIÉRREZ

Following the rally at 26 Federal Plaza, Congressman Luis Gutiérrez of Illinois reached out to me to collaborate on immigration reform. The congressman had become the champion of immigration rights in the U.S. Congress. He also had just come off a rally in Chicago, called A Caravan of Hope for Immigration. He wanted to do a similar event in New York City, so he contacted NYS assemblyman José Rivera of the Bronx, then the Bronx county leader, and asked him for a leader in the religious community. The assemblyman recommended me, and the congressman contacted me. I agreed to collaborate with him, and convened a meeting of religious leaders, including the Council of Hispanic Bishops and other religious organizations.

Congressman Gutiérrez and other elected officials met with the group, and we planned a second rally of the church leaders, which we held at La Sinagoga on 125th Street in East Harlem. The congressman was the keynote speaker and spoke to over 2,000 church leaders. A year later, he joined the group of NYC Latino Pentecostal evangelicals to hold a rally at LPAC's headquarters in the Bronx, the Urban Ministry Complex. This rally was held to maintain the energy around immigration reform, and to get people to the March on Washington, of which he was an organizer. Over seven hundred people attended, and again, Congressman Gutiérrez was the speaker of honor.

Be Light and Salt When Engaging Systems and Structures

Ultimately, the goal of engaging the powers is to improve the conditions in the community. As I mentioned above, some Christians still question whether God gives his people permission to engage the powers, but by now I hope you have seen that God has called his people to work with, and within, the system. Of course, this does not diminish the sufficiency of God, which I affirm as revealed to us in the Bible. But it is an exercise in self-denial to reject the notion that God has used his people to work with those outside of the covenant community to serve his purposes. It is impossible to deny that God's people have been light and salt despite the often challenging circumstances of captivity.

Interestingly, God allows captivity to come: "Thus says the Lord of hosts, the God of Israel, to all who were carried away captive, whom I have caused to be carried away from Jerusalem to Babylon . . ." (Jeremiah 29:4). In the midst of this reality, he invites his people to be light and salt as they deal with the powers. In fact, it was in the midst of captivity that the three Hebrew youths and Daniel were inducted into civil service as governors. In Esther's case, the decree of the civil authority to bring women into the palace enabled Esther, an orphaned, adopted captive, to become queen (Esther 2:17).

In Joseph's case, imprisonment facilitated his eventual rise within the Egyptian civil structure. Joseph then used his God-given gift of interpretation of dreams to provide guidance and direction to Pharaoh (Genesis 40:1-36). Subsequently, Pharaoh empowered Joseph to formulate and direct public policy over the fourteen years of plenty and famine. He also made Joseph second in command of the entire empire (41:37-56).

In Babylon, after giving King Nebuchadnezzar guidance, direction, wisdom, and knowledge, Daniel and the three Hebrew youths became governors over certain provinces (Daniel 2:46-49). In Persia, King Ahasuerus extended control and authority to Mordecai over the empire's resources (Esther 8:2). He also permitted Esther and Mordecai to change his policy as it related to the destruction of God's covenant community (8:8-10). Later, the king made Mordecai second in command over the entire empire (10:3). In Palestine, after receiving a vision, Peter engaged Cornelius, a Roman centurion (Acts 10:1-32). After being saved, Cornelius came to serve God's Kingdom.

While God's people may receive individual benefits from engaging the powers, they ultimately are serving a higher, liberating cause. As they do so, God calls his people to engage within the societal norms. "Seek the welfare [shalom] of the city" (Jeremiah 29:4-7). "Render to Caesar the things that are Caesar's" (Matthew 22:21). "Obey your leaders and submit to them" (Hebrews 13:17). Thus, Mordecai reports an assassination plot against King Ahasuerus (Esther 2:19-23). At the same time, God calls his people to work alongside the powers to reflect Kingdom values, regardless of whether the results are sustainable.

BRONX BOROUGH PRESIDENT FERNANDO FERRER

This has been the case as I have engaged the powers and their agents, including Bronx Borough President Fernando Ferrer. Our relationship developed over his tenure as borough president, gradually moving beyond one of a constituent with an elected official and becoming much more personal and friendly. I attended many official meetings as a spiritual leader in the Bronx, where we interacted on policy and program issues. He also attended, at my invitation, meetings with pastors and bishops in our religious community to explain his vision for the Bronx.

Ferrer and I went on to face several crises together, including the deaths of Anthony Baez and Amadou Diallo in the 1990s. Both shook the social fabric of the Bronx and of the rest of New York City and became symbols of the community's disenfranchisement and marginalization by our city's political powers. Everyone expected riots to break out in our communities when the judicial system handed down not-guilty verdicts for the police officers involved. Because of these concerns, I engaged the borough president and had a part in his handling of these shootings.

In the 1994 death of Anthony Baez, Ferrer was perceived as not doing enough, even though he called for an investigation. I rallied the Bronx Clergy Task Force, which held several press conferences denouncing the police and the city administration. We also supported Baez's mother at the trial with public prayer. We asked Ferrer to call out for justice by using his "bully pulpit" to denounce this act of police brutality. There I was in the midst of it all, helping to establish an alliance of Latin Kings, Nietas, New Black Panthers Party, New Young Lords Party, Communist Party, Socialist Party, and other political and community groups. We held community meetings at LPAC and demonstrated at the courthouse. Ultimately, Ferrer spoke out against the actions of the officers.

In the 1999 shooting of Amadou Diallo by police officers, Ferrer was so concerned that he gathered a group of ministers under my leadership. I already was active in the Bronx Clergy Task Force, so I initiated prayer and peace rallies to prepare for a turbulent time in our community. On the afternoon of the Diallo verdict, Ferrer invited us into his office and asked us to pray for the peace of the Bronx. His concern was that the Bronx would burn and that all that had been accomplished there during his tenure would be destroyed.

That evening, the clergy walked the streets with him. As the people heard the verdict of "not guilty" they came out of their homes spontaneously. The police were out in full force. I remember vividly the clashes and the shoving between police and community members. The clergy was in the middle, trying to keep the scuffles from escalating and deteriorating into physical confrontation. There was a group of outside agitators, professional radicals that wanted violence to occur. They were doing everything possible to clash with police. I, along with other members of the clergy, stood our ground shoulder to shoulder, acting as mediators, even putting ourselves at risk. In the end, the Bronx did not burn, which I attribute in part to the power of prayer. Later, Ferrer established a chaplain's commission to respond to emergencies in the community, and he appointed me its chair.

U.S. Congressman José Serrano

Another system agent whom I have engaged is U.S. Congressman José Serrano. Over the years, Rep. Serrano and I have connected on issues of immigration, housing, education, environmental justice, and the U.S. Navy occupation of the Puerto Rican island of Vieques. In the process, I have educated the congressman on how public policy issues, such as morality, war, and poverty, affected our Christian and community constituencies. We built a friendship based on mutual respect, which resulted in the ability to work together even when we disagreed on issues. Along the way, I helped him access the leadership of our community. In the process, he got to share his views with us, even when we disagreed.

On one occasion, the congressman approached me to host a meeting between him and President Hugo Chávez of Venezuela. At the time, Chávez was being accused of being a socialist, even a communist. People were saying that he was moving his country toward dictatorship and that he had anti-American sentiments. They also accused him of trying to control and monopolize his country's oil resources, which was having a drastic effect on the price of fuel in the United States and other nations. Too many in the Cuban community were angry because of his relationship with Fidel Castro. Chávez said that he considered Castro his mentor, but he said he was not a communist. He said he was a Christian and believed in a new socialism for the twenty-first century.

Congressman Serrano wanted to learn about Chávez's new policies for Venezuela and his views on the direction Latin America should take in the coming years. I myself saw Chávez as someone who was exploring alternatives for his country. The truth is that over the past century U.S. foreign policy has sometimes supported dictators and others in Latin America who have not benefited their people, often because of the U.S.'s national security interests. In these instances, the rich have continued to get richer and the poor have gotten poorer. So I did not see anything wrong with what Chávez was doing. I simply saw it as part of a struggle that he was embarked on for justice in his own country.

After the congressman approached me, many people, including other elected officials and religious leaders, said they did not think my hosting Chávez was a good thing. "It will stigmatize you," they warned. "The U.S. government would not be too happy with it. You receive public funds." I acknowledged their concerns, but after meeting with bishops and other leaders several times I convinced them to participate, and they were able to share their views at the meeting. I also reminded my leadership, both at LPAC and the Sanctuary Church, and everyone involved within my networks, that our responsibility is to the whole world. Besides, here was an opportunity for us to gain access to Chávez and ask questions. And Serrano, I felt, was a man of integrity, particularly in the context of foreign policy, and he always supported the oppressed and marginalized in his legislation. He also had supported community programs.

So I held the event in our gymnasium, and it was an incredible experience. The community-based activist community was there. The political community was there, too. The religious community was also there, as Serrano wanted Chávez to have access to them.[2]

All week long, FBI and other intelligence agents were stationed at LPAC. Venezuelan security met with me and others to work out the logistics. The place was packed. The press was out in full force. People wanted to get in at all costs. There were lines, even though the event was by invitation only. In the end, I was able to equip my leadership to deal with issues that were greater than the local setting, even if they were controversial. I accepted the challenge and worked with the congressman so that my community could interact with people and issues that were affecting the rest of the world, especially Latin America and the Caribbean.

NYC HUMAN RESOURCES ADMINISTRATION

In addition to engaging individual system agents of the powers, I have been able to serve as light and salt to entire agencies. In 2002, I engaged

2. Interestingly, in Venezuela, the Pentecostal and evangelical community reportedly was very supportive of Chávez's initiatives because they had benefited the poor through schools in poor areas, health clinics, and literacy programs for the poor. In unofficial grassroots circles, he received good press. At the same time, many in the country's dominant press vilified him.

the Temporary Assistance for Needy Families (TANF) program of the NYC Human Resources Administration (HRA). TANF was part of HRA's work-related project called "workfare," in which recipients had to work for their checks. TANF aimed to empower, equip, train, and counsel welfare recipients, who were at the bottom of the system. Some participants felt that the program had them working for slave wages, and they wondered why they couldn't at least be hired at a decent wage. While I agreed with this view to some degree, I opened LPAC's doors with the hope of speaking life to them and empowering them in some way.

Because TANF was not able to contact this population, it subcontracted to LPAC to reach out to them, under the assumption that the church could relate to them in a non-adversarial way — especially because many saw HRA as the enemy. So we took on this task and its baggage. In particular, we became responsible for reaching out to those individuals who had violated all the rules and regulations, did not go to meetings, and would not respond to letters. These men and women were about to be eliminated from the rolls.

To some, we seemed to have become agents of the powers, because we were enforcing the rules. Yet we contacted the people through personal, door-to-door visits, and they finally came in. I remember the first morning of the program. The overwhelming majority who came were women. I was struck by the sadness on their faces; there was no sparkle in their eyes. They seemed totally discouraged and depressed. I quickly realized that they were the victims of the powers, which were brutal and dehumanizing. Many would come into LPAC with attitudes of anger and hostility because they saw us collaborating with people who had little regard for them. Many were anticipating that we would disrespect them as human beings and treat them as if they had no value.

I remember drawing on biblical lessons and truths to assure them that we were not there to accuse them: "He who is without sin among you, let him throw a stone at her first" (John 8:7). We stressed that we were not there to judge them. They were not there to be beaten up. In fact, we wanted to speak life into them. We wanted them to know that they did have potential and were made in the image and likeness of God. We wanted to see them use their gifts and talents to have new beginnings and opportunities. Fortunately, many responded. After just one day with us, I noticed a sparkle in many of their eyes and a spring in their walk. They seemed to believe again that change was possible. I felt good about engaging the powers because I was able to bring the people into compliance — not because compliance for its own sake is necessarily good, but because in this case compliance enabled them to survive while they sought these better opportunities.

I even accompanied some of these women to the welfare offices and advocated for them. The atmosphere of control and coercion and manipulation there was so extreme that people felt like nothing. The system devalued them. And after years, or even short periods of time, they just gave up and became numbers. They were treated with profound disrespect. When I accompanied them, they were treated with a measure of respect because I was a member of the clergy. But when they were alone, they were just seen, whether unconsciously or subconsciously, as subhuman, as people who lived off the system and did not deserve to be treated with dignity and self-respect.

All told, LPAC registered program participants at their local TANF center, gave them job-readiness skills, and assisted them with job placement. During the year and a half that the program was in effect, we exceeded the milestones set by NYC HRA, having served over 320 clients. Over half of the participants served had their sanctions lifted because of our involvement. Many had a sparkle back in their eyes. The program helped them to believe again that change was possible.

NYC DEPARTMENT OF CORRECTIONS

In the late 2000s, the NYC Department of Corrections became another agency I engaged. I became an advocate for inmates who were facing dehumanizing conditions. This involved meeting with the commissioner and officers and developing a program for people visiting prisoners through the department's Alternative to Incarceration program. The program director was a Muslim imam. I felt strange about this at first: here the majority of the people of color were Christians, but an imam was directing the department.

While I always prided myself on being an ecumenical and interfaith person, I wondered to myself why he was in that position. But God has a way of confusing us. The imam had, I learned, come out of a Christian tradition and was very receptive to Christians. He understood our tradition and spoke the language of faith, salvation, and personal transformation. So he reached out to me, which opened the doors for us to enter into the prisons. He came out to LPAC and held orientation sessions to teach us how to work within a prison setting. He was very cooperative and collaborative.

Nevertheless, I was ambivalent. I vacillated because I knew that the prison system, as it was organized, was punitive in nature and very little if any rehabilitation went on. But through my relationship with the imam, we were able to establish a pilot program that we have operated in-kind for over two years.

As a result, we have provided support services to the inmates through our in-kind Prison Faith Reentry Project. As a partnership between the Sanctuary Church and LPAC, we deployed several of our church and LPAC staff members to visit Riker's Island Correctional Facility, one of the most densely populated prisons in the United States, to meet weekly with male and female inmates. Then, after inmates complete their sentences, we connect them to churches in their community. In turn, these churches assist them with support and resources that have helped them transition effectively into the mainstream society.

On a related note, we have provided the in-kind Community Service Program, which enables adjudicated youth at least fourteen years old to complete sixty hours of community service at LPAC. These young people have been found guilty by the system but receive a second chance through our program. We counsel the youth and give them meaningful and constructive tasks that help them develop transferable job and personal skills. To date, dozens of youth have completed the program and have stopped behaviors that bring them before the juvenile justice system.

Secure Support to Advance Community Initiatives

When you engage the powers, you have the potential to access financial, material, and human resources to serve the body of Christ and the society at large. At times, the church has lacked the resources to carry out its peace and justice mission, so it has partnered with the powers. We can see this engagement bearing fruit in the U.S. and abroad in the building of hospitals, schools, and orphanages.

Think back to the story of Nehemiah. His engagement yielded resources for Jerusalem and his community of origin, the covenant community. Before Nehemiah became involved in Jerusalem's state of affairs, Ezra the priest, who had been in Jerusalem twelve years before Nehemiah, admitted being ashamed to ask the king for help:

For I was ashamed to request of the king an escort of soldiers and horsemen to help us against the enemy on the road, because we had spoken to the king, saying, "The hand of our God is upon all those for good who seek Him, but His power and His wrath are against all those who forsake Him." (Ezra 8:22)

However, Nehemiah was not ashamed to ask King Artaxerxes for resources that would benefit the covenant community.

After the king saw him sad, Nehemiah was able to share his concern:

I said to the king, "May the king live forever! Why should my face not be sad, when the city, the place of my fathers' tombs, lies waste, and its gates are burned with fire?" (Nehemiah 2:3)

In turn, the king asked Nehemiah what he needed from him, and Nehemiah prayed. With the clarity of God's wisdom, Nehemiah respectfully revealed his vision for Jerusalem and made a formal request for resources (2:7-8). Clearly Nehemiah understood that God was directing his steps and was opening the doors and the hearts of the system agents.

Over the years, I have received ministry support from city, state, and federal agencies. I will be the first to say that these funds have been a mixed bag. On the one hand, they have enabled us to provide many community programs. On the other hand, I have been under constant scrutiny to ensure I did not engage in any "inherently" religious activity. Our programs are open to everyone, regardless of religious affiliation. Yet some of their ministries have inherently Kingdom-oriented goals. Thus, I have had to strike a balance between spiritual and secular ministries. This has posed a challenge because I have always sought to provide holistic services, which combine the spiritual with the emotional, mental, physical, and social. While I upheld my contractual obligations and kept things separate, I cannot lie and say that this did not bring about tension in me.

There have been times when I have declined to solicit funds because I believed they would restrict my ability to provide holistic ministries. While this may have reduced our overall funding for community programs, I was confident that I could secure resources to operate these programs without restrictions being placed on them by the powers. And I never felt it would advance the mission of the ministries I was operating to stop soliciting resources altogether. Like Nehemiah, I was confident that God opens the coffers of the state to provide for his people and to realize his plans for restoration and redemption.

NYC DIRECTOR OF HISPANIC AFFAIRS
JOSEPH ERAZO

It was with this perspective that I engaged Joseph Erazo, the Director of Hispanic Affairs under Mayor Abraham Beame. It was the early 1970s, a time full of controversy. It was the aftermath of the 1960s, and there was a radical perspective in many of the communities, a legacy of such influences as the Black Panthers, the Young Lords, the Students for a Democratic Society, and the Vietnam War. Print and other media reported constantly about African Americans and Puerto Ricans and their plight. Crime was high. Unemployment was high. Tensions were high in the community.[3]

By this time I was organizing within my community and had received a certain amount of public recognition, both as a pastor and as someone who had access to resources and power. I had begun to be part of citywide coalitions that were advocating for the Puerto Rican community to get its fair share of resources and funds. There was a sense that the African American community had a disproportionate amount of the resources; yet, if truth be told, the resources were not enough for any community. The powers had manipulated communities into fighting for crumbs, which was the state of people of color at that time.[4] We found their actions to be sinful, so we raised our voices against them.

It was through this that I developed a relationship with Mr. Erazo. I told him about the large collective leadership of the Pentecostal church. I pointed to recent news articles about the phenomenon of storefront Pen-

3. I gained a better understanding of the relationship between race, power, Christianity, and the poor from James Cone. I learned how these factors played themselves out in everyday existence. I also understood how Christians of color perceived themselves, including their identity, and how they viewed the white dominant church. Thus, in my relationship with elected officials, I appreciated that they dealt with me based on the power they perceived I had through my church constituency. The books by James Cone that impacted me were the following: *A Black Theology of Liberation* (Maryknoll, NY: Orbis Books, 1970); and *Black Theology and Black Power* (New York: Seabury Press, 1969).

4. This is another example of Cone's view that race, power, and economics are interrelated. Also it reveals the role of the dominant white culture and church in this reality.

tecostal churches, and how they had begun to take over synagogues and supermarkets and renovate these buildings. These churches were exploding. There were maybe two thousand Pentecostal churches in the city, and they were growing at a phenomenal rate. The dominant culture was taking note.

In turn, Mr. Erazo told me about resources that were available to combat poverty, so I convened a meeting of leaders of Pentecostal and other denominational churches, including Methodists, Disciples of Christ, Lutherans, Evangelicals, and Baptists. Subsequently, we formed Acción Cívica Evangélica (Civic Evangelical Action), which became the largest Pentecostal evangelical nonprofit group formed in New York City up until that time. Then, through Mr. Erazo's advocacy, we accessed funding from the city. Of course, this did not stop us from confronting the city's administration when it was not being responsive to the Puerto Rican community in other areas.

Through this relationship, Acción Cívica received several contracts: a summer youth employment contract from the Department of Labor, a manpower contract from the Department of Employment, and a senior citizens contract from the Department of the Aging. We also received funding for infrastructure. On the strength of these local contracts, we also received a summer lunch program contract from the U.S. Department of Agriculture. Ultimately, we were administering a budget of millions of dollars, with a staff of thirty to forty people.

NYS ASSEMBLYMAN ANGELO DEL TORO

In the early 1980s, I served as the executive assistant of NYS Assemblyman Angelo Del Toro in East Harlem. This brought me into a new arena because, after leaving the Reformed Church in America, I did not want to be in full-time ministry. But I still wanted to serve people, and this new role gave me the opportunity to do that. The assemblyman hired me after he saw me at a Manhattan School District 4 function at the Manhattan Center for Science and Math, in which I created a recognition ceremony supported by Governor Mario Cuomo. Over two thousand clergy and their congregations attended, which served to honor our community leaders.

This function coincided with the assemblyman running for president of the New York City Council, a citywide office. He saw my convening power, my power to organize and mobilize people. So he hired me, and I served as his bridge to the religious and community organizing communities. I remember him looking to me to help him navigate these two communities, which were significant players in East Harlem.

Almost immediately I became a trusted member of his inner circle. Even though I was not an experienced political operative, Del Toro recognized that I had stayed close and connected to my constituency. He dealt with me respectfully because he knew that behind me were hundreds of churches that supported my perspective. Thus, he treated me with a certain amount of status.

Through my convening power, the assemblyman gained access to the Puerto Rican Hispanic Pentecostal Evangelical community. I did a tour with him, in which he spoke at every major religious Pentecostal council in the city. He became a household name among them and they began to develop relationships with him. He met with bishops and with every Christian ministry and program. He even gained access to hundreds of pulpits and pastors in New York City. He engaged Christian communities in policy discussions and in delivering services to his constituencies. I also connected him to leaders of community organizing movements, and they were able to dialogue and worked together on formulating pro-community public policies.

As I worked for the assemblyman and engaged systemic sin from the inside, I did so in the context of my community. I was not a maverick. I did not act as an individual. Like Joseph in Egypt, Daniel in Babylon, and Nehemiah and Esther in Persia, all of whom worked directly for the powers, I gained a particular insight into the inner workings of power and legislation, and resources and funding. This enhanced my ability to equip the saints as I stayed connected to my community.

I shared with them how laws were passed, how legislation was created, and how coalitions were made. Because Del Toro was chairman of the black and Puerto Rican legislative caucus, which encompassed every African American and Latino elected official, I was able to give them an inner view of political power, as well as systemic power and sin, and how their priorities were determined. I also showed them how we should advocate prophetically for those issues and those programs that were aligned with the Kingdom of God.

CHARTER SCHOOL INSTITUTE (CSI)

Along with individual system agents of the powers, I also secured support from entire agencies. For example, in 2000, I took advantage of the new charter school law in New York State and applied for a charter school through the Charter School Institute (CSI), a collaboration of the state, the Board of Regents, and the State University of New York. I saw it as an opportunity to submit an application for a charter school that was aligned with my vision of proving that English language learners could learn in a district that was functioning far below the other parts of the city and the country. For this initiative, I led a team of community and education leaders to secure a charter school license under the State of New York Alternative School Program. This committee included educators and people who I felt represented our community and could clearly articulate our vision and mission to the State Department of Education.

In 2001, we submitted an application and began navigating that system. We met with CSI officials and asked them to provide us the guidelines, support, and resources so that we could meet the criteria for a charter school. We insisted that our vision was to work with English language learners, but CSI said we had to work with everyone, regardless of their English proficiency. Part of its feedback was that we could not exclude anyone from the community, that we could not exclude other groups from our charter. We continued to insist that our vision was for a charter school for English language learners, and we stood firm on that. It was nonnegotiable.

In addition, CSI told us that our students would have to meet the same standards that everyone else did. We argued that English language learners took more time to acquire the language, but they said there would be no exceptions. We fought over that issue for a long time and at different meetings, but we eventually told them that we did not want it to be used as an excuse. And while there was always tension in our relationship with this agent of the powers, we wanted them to understand the context of English language learners when reviewing our application. At least we all agreed that raising standards for our population was a good thing.

In the end, we agreed to accept everyone. But we remained committed to focusing on English language learners, establishing recruitment policies that would ensure a high enrollment of these students. At the same time, I warned CSI that one day their refusal to let us officially focus on English language learners would come back to haunt them. Unfortunately or fortunately, depending on your perspective, my words turned out to be prophetic; ten years later this is the greatest criticism of charter schools in the state and nation.

The first year, our proposal was rejected. Then, in 2002, CSI awarded us a five-year charter to operate the Family Life Academy Charter School (FLACS). As FLACS's community sponsor, LPAC provided the vision and framework through which the school would operate. We also provided guidance on particular issues, as we see FLACS as one of the most important building blocks of our local community. The K-8 school is housed at LPAC's headquarters and prepares over four hundred children to achieve high standards, take responsibility for their own learning, and explore and affirm human values. In addition, CSI approved our charter with an emphasis on English language learners. As a result of our recruitment strategies, FLACS now represents the majority of these students within the state's charter school system.

FLACS has provided the state the opportunity to partner with a community-grown charter school. This has created the vehicle for the state to be in direct relationship with a faith-based community organization and created an ongoing dynamic where the principles of the community sponsor would impact the way the state would promote public education. Presently, FLACS is functioning extremely well, and CSI is hailing it as a model for quality public education. Indeed, the success of FLACS serves as proof that Christian community ministries can partner effectively with government institutions and produce quality education for children whom the system has historically failed to educate. In September 2012, FLACS II opened in the Bronx to offer quality education to a new crop of children and families.

Corporation for National and Community Service

A few years later, in 2004, I sought the support of the Corporation for National and Community Service (CNCS), the federal agency that runs AmeriCorps. I navigated the federal bureaucracy to launch the National Urban Ministry Project (NUMP), which was a capacity building and direct service partnership of five faith-based organizations across the United States: LPAC in the Bronx; Ayuda Community Center in Philadelphia; La Capilla del Barrio in Chicago; My Friend's House in Whittier,

California; and Spanish Evangelical Church in Lawrence, Massachusetts. This was during the administration of President George W. Bush, and not surprisingly, those in our community who did not see the Bush administration in a positive light accused me of being in cahoots with a conservative Republican administration.

However, through NUMP, I helped our partners develop their local communities by guiding youth and adults to a lifelong calling of personal and community growth. In the process, our partners developed programs and activities for children, youth, and adults, along with tools to measure the effectiveness of these programs. Some launched or expanded their after-school programs and youth development programs, and some created adult and family-based programs. Throughout, we provided technical assistance and guidance to ensure formal and informal connections and shared-learning opportunities among the sites, including conference calls.

Manage Internal and External Tensions

As I have engaged the powers, I have sometimes had to deal with system agents who were not part of the initial relationship we established. At times, these agents have become obstacles. Some have lacked the spirit of excellence in their service, whether through choice or lack of preparation. Others have lacked empathy, after years of conditioning by the fallen civil authority. In its place, they may have a spirit of apathy, callousness, and resentment toward the people they are paid to serve.

Some lack a spirit of hospitality, which is revealed when they do not welcome people, making those who come to them feel as if they are being done a favor instead of being served. Undoubtedly this makes people feel that they really would prefer them not to be there. Furthermore, some abuse and misuse their power, using it for personal benefit and to distinguish between people and discriminate against them. Some promote and extend opportunities to others based not on their qualifications or specific criteria, but on questions of power and influence. Extreme cases include sexual harassment and selected nitpicking of individuals.

In addition, the powers will at times ask you to act in a way that is contrary to your God-given call. As a fallen entity, the powers maintain a culture, norms, and decrees that are not rooted in Kingdom values. Thus, you must recognize God's law and behave in accordance with it. This often puts you at tension with the system agent or agency. In fact, your actions may put you on a collision course with the powers. You may go in another direction, speaking against the prevailing powers' culture, when the expectation is to submit and to fall in line. You may even conclude that you no longer can submit or bow to a particular cultural expectation or norm, even if it puts you in harm's way.

Again, the Scriptures bear this out in the case of Daniel and the three Hebrew youths during the Babylonian captivity. The three young men worked for the powers, but they simply would not bow to the golden statue, even at the risk of being cast into the fiery furnace (Daniel 3:16). At another point, Daniel prayed with his windows open at the risk of being thrown into the lions' den (6:10). During the Persian captivity, Queen Esther went to the king even though she had "not been called to come in to the king these thirty days" (Esther 4:11).

What's more, the powers at times feed on each other, compete with each other, and even consume each other. Gridlock is often the order of the day, in which authentic communication does not take place. The powers may ask you to take sides. It is here where you must navigate these tensions and maximize your relationships. You must be at peace that you will not fully solve the broader issues of personal and institutional decay. You will see the contradictions in places like the prison system, where the polarization between guards and prisoners has led to riots and deaths. Here, your task is to facilitate dialogue and communication, even if you do not bring about full reconciliation or better living and working conditions.

NEW YORK STATE SENATOR PEDRO ESPADA

This was the situation when I engaged former Majority Leader of the New York State Senate, Pedro Espada. At the time I worked with him, Senator Espada was being vilified in the press and accused of stealing funds. But he had not been indicted or convicted of any crime. So when he spoke out on immigration, I supported him. When he spoke out against violence to young people and the gay community, I supported him. Not surprisingly, this relationship caused me tension with fellow activists, as they saw him as a political hack and one who did not deserve any support. Some perceived him to be arrogant or aloof and to be looking out only for himself. The press or political enemies also vilified him.

But it was the price I was willing to pay in order to influence the passage of laws and policies that were aligned with Kingdom values and ultimately would serve the neediest citizens of the state. I also felt compelled to provide prayer during his ordeal.

NYC Human Resources Administration

I faced a similar tension when I ran the TANF program of the NYC Human Resources Administration. As you may recall, the men and women we were serving had been the victims of a system that was deeply insensitive to them. At the welfare offices, the workers would be extremely disrespectful until they learned I was with the clients. Afterwards, many of them would become more responsive, and even respectful. With me, they figured that they were dealing with someone who had power and authority. Yet when the clients would go alone again, they would find themselves once again treated unfairly. In contrast, our staff treated them with respect and dignity. That is why so many were animated about actively responding to the program requirements.

Corporation for National and Community Service

Yet another tension I faced was with the Corporation for National and Community Service (CNCS) in regard to LPAC's National Urban Ministry Project. There I was in the midst of the Bush administration, with which I disagreed on almost all policy issues. I was against its foreign policy, its war in Iraq, its concept of first strikes, and the "macho" military image it seemed to want to project in the world. I also disagreed with its economic policy of tax breaks for the rich. Yet while most of my friends were activists aligned against this administration, I chose to partner with its faith-based initiative. Through LPAC, I was opening doors for many other faith-based organizations, so I was willing to fight the good fight to preserve this vital issue for the faith community.

At the same time, I recognized that, although President Bush supported faith-based programs in his rhetoric, the policies at a middle-management bureaucracy level effectively remained the same. So, as CNCS officials met with me, they tried to deter me from having a faith perspective. But I was unapologetically Christ-centered, and yet I did not seek to proselytize or convert people to my own religion through this initiative. As a practitioner of holistic ministry, I was involved in community development because of my faith. I was not about to deny that. So I addressed the double-standard that faith-based programs could not maintain a faith perspective in their programming.

As I mentioned before, CNCS initially did not want us to use the term "ministry," which we successfully argued simply meant "service." At the same time, we did have to change the title of NUMP members from "urban missionaries" to "urban mission specialists" because CNCS felt it had too much of a religious Christian connotation. In the end, we felt this was a minor concession, so we promptly changed the program materials accordingly. Yet we continued to articulate our faith connection internally. This enabled the members to apply our methodology effectively.

NYC DEPARTMENT OF CORRECTIONS

In working with the NYC Department of Corrections, I had to deal with the fact that people had to travel for hours just to get to the Rikers Island Correctional Facility. Mothers, wives, and children had difficulty visiting their family members, which increased the isolation, disconnection, and marginalization of the inmates. It also was very difficult for inmates to get access to lawyers because lawyers did not want to make the trip. Subsequently, I engaged the commissioner and connected him to other religious leaders. To me, God's purpose for prisoners was to be closer to their community, and even in their communities.

On a related matter, I invited the commissioner to LPAC to speak at our Faith and Public Life Speakers Series. He wanted to build a prison to alleviate the overcrowding at Rikers. This produced a tremendous reaction from the community: *One more prison in the Bronx?* The community felt, *Here goes the system, the principalities and powers again, dumping things that no one wants in their white communities into communities of color.* They compared it to making our community a toxic waste dump, since, as they saw it, there were already so many other negative things in our community.

Yet I believed the commissioner genuinely wanted to alleviate the overcrowding at Rikers and improve the prison environment there. I also saw this as a way to improve access for families, legal professionals, and service providers. So I connected him to the faith community, to have a hearing with them and to explain his motivation. He met with several bishops in our community, who supported his plan.

Yet at the official hearing of community groups, the meeting was polarized. Most were against the prison, including some of my friends and fellow activists. Meanwhile, the faith leaders were on the other side saying that the prison in our community was a good idea. I felt that it was God's purpose for prisoners to be closer to their community, and even in their communities. That way, we could provide more support to them. We saw this initiative as aligned with Kingdom values, so we engaged the powers despite some public opposition.

Indeed, as I engaged the powers, I have been astonished at how receptive many have been to my voice. Even as I maintained the prophetic content of my message, they reacted soberly to it. They even gained insight to the particular issues in which we were engaged. I always felt a sense of respect despite there having been the potential for conflict. I can honestly say that engaging the powers produced concrete change in public policy, led to funding priorities that reflect Kingdom values, and contributed to the voiceless gaining access to the halls of power. I hope sharing these experiences will help you envision ways that God may be calling you to engage the powers.

CHAPTER 7

You Can Confront the Powers!

૮ฬ૰

A s you may have realized, the powers work tirelessly to indoctrinate
their citizens into the values of the kingdom of man. Their secularism perpetuates faithlessness and a self-centered way of life. In many
ways, the church has not discerned the true nature of the powers, and
thus has not provided a prophetic voice in response to their philosophies
and actions. Regrettably, the church at times has emulated the ways of
the powers. Yet where others have seen beauty, splendor, and grandiosity
in the powers and their empires, I have discerned ugliness and deceit,
camouflaged in generosity.

Indeed, I have seen the true identity behind the images of gold, silver,
bronze, iron, and clay. Fortunately, God revealed through Daniel the reality of the powers:

> This image's head was of fine gold, its chest and arms of silver, its
> belly and thighs of bronze, its legs of iron, its feet partly of iron and
> partly of clay. You watched while a stone was cut out without hands,
> which struck the image on its feet of iron and clay, and broke them in
> pieces. Then the iron, the clay, the bronze, the silver, and the gold
> were crushed together, and became like chaff from the summer
> threshing floors; the wind carried them away so that no trace of
> them was found. And the stone that struck the image became a great
> mountain and filled the whole earth. (Daniel 2:32-35)

Through Daniel's interpretation of Babylonian King Nebuchadnezzar's
dream (2:36-44), we learn about four different kingdoms that are repre-

116

sented by the statue (Babylon, Medo-Persia, Greece, and Rome). And while these kingdoms may appear different in some respects, in their essence they basically are the same in that they strive to conquer other peoples.

Indeed, the book of Daniel offers us more insights into the true nature of the powers. Not long after Daniel interpreted his dream, King Nebuchadnezzar ordered all citizens to worship his image:

> Then a herald cried aloud: "To you it is commanded, O peoples, nations, and languages, that at the time you hear the sound of the horn, flute, harp, lyre, and psaltery, in symphony with all kinds of music, you shall fall down and worship the gold image that King Nebuchadnezzar has set up." (3:4-5)

Failure to comply with the decree would result in being "cast into a burning fiery furnace" (3:6). Eventually, enemies of God's covenant community informed the king that three Hebrew youths — Shadrach, Meshach, and Abednego — were not abiding by the decree (3:8-12). In response, the king confronted them and reminded them of the penalty for their defiance (3:13-15). In turn, the young men lifted up God as their deliverer and told the king they would not serve his gods or worship the golden image (3:17-18).

Sure enough, the king cast them into the burning fiery furnace (3:19-23). You probably know what happened next. A fourth figure appeared in the midst of the fire and saved the three Hebrew youths. Then, after the men survived the furnace, King Nebuchadnezzar worshiped the "God of Shadrach, Meshach, and Abednego." He even wrote a decree that honored the one true God, and he promoted the three Hebrew youths to positions of honor (3:25-30). Indeed, their faithfulness was instrumental in their deliverance and advancement.

Yet while the powers seek obedience and honor, they have failed to meet the needs of their citizens. They have perpetrated brutality and dehumanization. In our own day, increasingly punitive laws are enacted for blue-collar crimes. Public schools are failing mostly low-income and ethnic-minority students. Prisons are filled up mostly with African Americans, Latinos, and poor whites. The healthcare system downplays preventative care. The citizens with the highest incomes are receiving the greatest tax advantages. Social services have been drastically reduced. Predatory and deceitful lending institutions sell unaffordable mortgages. These and other social policies have been maintained through the powers' laws and traditions. Regrettably, these satanic manifestations have become institutionalized within the powers' prevailing systems and structures.

These abuses have led to poverty, hunger, violence, and sickness around the world. Many people have lost their dignity, intrinsic self-worth, and ability to make their own decisions. Historically, this has prompted the church to confront the powers and influence them to be aligned with Kingdom values and to adopt socially just policies. In the process, God's people have drawn from their collective identity to confront the powers and bring about peace and justice in the midst of captivity.

Given this reality, God may be calling you to be today's Moses. As you may recall, Moses confronted the Egyptian establishment by declaring to Pharaoh on behalf of God, "Let my people go" (Exodus 5:1). Thus, you may voice your demands at a local school board meeting to ensure that schools help children meet national educational standards. You may organize a demonstration at City Hall to protest unreasonable laws. You may meet with bank officials to discuss unfair lending practices related to mortgages and small business loans. You may join a media campaign aimed at regulatory agencies to advocate local control of the media rather than control by conglomerates.

Of course, you should expect today's Pharaohs to reject the voice of God. Do not be surprised if the powers continue to implement even more oppressive policies and practices to burden the people. Yet although some voices of conscience have been muted and ridiculed, others have contributed significantly to positive social change. This is why you should confront the powers. By doing so, you can openly challenge the powers. You can provide a prophetic voice. You can ensure that community needs are met. In the process, you can oppose efforts to indoctrinate the community. Remember that you stand on the shoulders of those who came before you — the "cloud of witnesses" that surrounds you (Hebrews 12:1). Always trust in the power of God and the collective support of the people in your midst.

Openly Challenge the Powers

Throughout history, God's people have confronted the powers in response to the abuses perpetrated by the powers and their systems and structures. In fact, the church historically has caused the powers to be aligned authentically with Kingdom values. Whether it was the abolition of slavery, women's suffrage, workers' rights, civil rights, women's rights, voting rights, the rights of the unborn, or the promotion of national and community service, God's people have been at the vanguard of major Kingdom-minded social movements. They have influenced the powers to respond to the needs of the people and communities affected by the lack of pro-social policies. I pray that God lets me live to see the passing of other Kingdom-minded reforms around social services, healthcare, immigration, criminal justice, and other issues.

In more recent times, God's people have risked their credibility and lives to stand up to abuses by the powers. Frederick Douglass, Charles G. Finney, and Lucretia Mott were leaders in the abolitionist movement. Susan B. Anthony and Martha Wright fought for women's suffrage. The black church and its leaders, including Rev. Dr. Martin Luther King Jr., fought for civil rights. Rev. Leon H. Sullivan fought for job training and an end to apartheid in South Africa. Cesar Chavez fought for labor rights. Present-day Christian leaders like Jim Wallis and Rev. Luis Cortes have sought immigration reform.

These godly people were connected and tied to their people and communities. They saw their reality as intrinsically woven into the plight of their people. Thus, Martin Luther King may have been studying at Boston University, but he was intrinsically connected to his congregation and community in Atlanta. Indeed, it was this connection to his people and their reality that prompted him to forsake his safety and speak for them.

I like to think that these men and women of God drew from the struggles of men and women in the Bible, who confronted the powers of their time in the midst of their captivity. For example, I think of the resistance by the Hebrew midwives during the Egyptian captivity. After the death of Joseph, who had been second in command in Egypt, a new king of Egypt arose who feared the increasing power of the people of Israel and made them work as slaves (Exodus 1:8-14).

Interestingly, this oppression only led to greater prosperity for God's people. In response, the king approached the Hebrew midwives and commanded them to murder the infant Hebrew boys:

> When you do the duties of a midwife for the Hebrew women and see them on the birthstools, if it is a son, you shall kill him, but if it is a daughter, then she shall live. (1:16)

But the Hebrew midwives resisted the Pharaoh's decree for genocide. God had given the women wisdom to confront the king, so they saved the male children. This led to the growth and strength of God's people (1:18-20). Then, the Pharaoh commanded,

> Every son who is born [to the Hebrews] you shall cast into the river, and every daughter you shall save alive. (1:22)

But Moses' parents resisted the king's decree, choosing instead to hide their newborn son and then send him down the river in a basket. This led to Moses becoming a prince of Egypt (2:2-10). It also moved him along the path to becoming the liberator of God's chosen people.

POVERTY

Early on in my ministry, I had become conscious of the unjust policies and laws that were hurting people of color and the poor in New York City. As a result, I joined the NYC Council Against Poverty and later helped launch the NYC Puerto Rican Council Against Poverty. It was the late 1960s, and John Lindsay was mayor. Lyndon B. Johnson was president, and the War on Poverty was being rolled out as the centerpiece of the nation's cities. In Sunset Park, Brooklyn, a high-poverty area, the Puerto Rican community was growing while the white population was undergoing "white flight." There was fear and suspicion of the "newcomers," with their strange language and customs. Puerto Ricans faced stereotypes of being the corner beer-drinking crowd and lazy welfare cheats.

In the midst of this situation, Mayor Lindsay established the NYC Council Against Poverty, an initiative of the city's Community Development Agency that was made responsible for developing public policy and distributing anti-poverty funds across the city. Every local community elected a board and appointed local representatives to the citywide council. I was appointed to the local board and selected to be the local representative to the citywide body.

At the same time, resources still were not reaching the citywide Puerto Rican community proportionately, so Puerto Ricans began organizing throughout the city to respond to their treatment. In Sunset Park many people were forming small, emerging groups, so I organized them into the Puerto Rican Hispanic Assembly of Sunset Park. Other groups were forming throughout the city, so we established a collaborative movement that we called the NYC Puerto Rican Council Against Poverty. (At that time, "Puerto Rican" was synonymous with "Latino" or "Hispanic.") Among the leaders were Ramón Vélez of the South Bronx Multi-Service Center and the Puerto Rican Day Parade, and Dr. Evelina López Antonetty, founder of the United Bronx Parents.

Right away, the Puerto Rican Council held a series of actions. We understood that engagement would have to take place over an extended period of time, at least a few days, applying constant pressure and ongoing interaction. I felt like Joshua, who led the seven-day march around the wall of Jericho until the wall fell (Joshua 6). One of the days, we took over the NYC Council's building, and some of the more militant members of our group resorted to violence. Some of us were even arrested.

The following day, over two hundred assembly members went to the old Board of Estimate to point out the inequities that Puerto Ricans faced in the distribution of resources in our community and city. I interrupted the meeting and declared that we were taking it over. Next, our members got up and I took over the meeting. We kept everyone in attendance in the building. The police threatened to arrest us if we did not open the doors. Those who stayed let the police in and thirty-seven leaders were arrested. Herman Badillo, the movement's pro bono lawyer, got us released on our own recognizance. As I mentioned before, the incident made the evening news. Today, you may be the one to point out iniquities your community faces.

IMMIGRATION REFORM

Over the decades, I have continued to challenge the powers on issues affecting my community. In the late 2000s, I became involved in the national agenda on immigration reform. The immigration issue had become the primary issue in the national Latino community, with very significant implications for the New York City Pentecostal evangelical community. A Pew national poll on immigration and the undocumented population in the Latino community stated that close to 37 percent of our membership was undocumented. Up to 15 percent of Pentecostal pastors were undocumented themselves.

The established powers have perpetuated the myth that everything wrong with this country is due to undocumented workers. The media, elected officials, and religious leaders have sometimes joined in this false depiction of this community. Their focus has been to scapegoat the undocumented worker — to demonize undocumented families as people who put a tax burden on our country because they are draining resources from the national economy, not paying taxes, and being a burden on our health care system. The truth is exactly the opposite. Still, it has resulted in a backlash against the undocumented community to the point where in New York City it has deteriorated into violence.

Several people have been hurt badly or even killed. Some have been attacked by mobs spewing all kinds of racial slurs. There has been anger and hostility toward this community that recalls the civil rights era in this country, when African Americans were singled out and hurt by the majority community. In many ways, immigrants have become the new "Negro" or the new "Single Female-Headed Household" of the early twenty-first century. All the social ills that plague our country are somehow the fault of undocumented workers. Even the established laws have a negative focus: deportation, dividing families, and denying children the right to an education, even though they have graduated with good grades from high schools and have been in this country from a very early age. What makes this worse is that many do not even speak Spanish, and thus they would be aliens and illegals in their former countries.

Aware of this reality, I joined a group of the collective indigenous leadership of the Pentecostal evangelical wing of the church. Together we organized an immigration rally in front of 26 Federal Plaza in lower Manhattan to protest the unfair treatment of immigrants. We agreed to resist the established power of media and other religious leaders in our community, particularly from the dominant white culture, as well as the national elected leaders, who were perpetuating the division and hostility in our communities. We were well aware that this would be the first time a mass meeting of primarily Latino Pentecostal evangelical Christians was being held in New York City that did not address "Religious Right" issues of family values, same-sex marriage, or abortion.

We had called the bishops and assured them that this was an issue we had to take a stand on. We shared with them the Pew statistics, and reminded them that many of our people paid tithes and offerings, and they needed our protection. We also contended that the government had no moral authority to divide families. We reminded them of Jesus' words that a man shall leave his father and mother to be united to his wife, to his family and subsequent children, and no one should separate them (Matthew 19:5). We also reminded them that the Bible was full of hundreds of exhortations to welcome the stranger and the immigrant and also the poor and oppressed, which many of these immigrants had become.

We put in calls to Christian Radio Vision and Radio New Song, which broadcasted twenty-four hours a day in our communities. We also contacted the newspaper *El Diario*. We went to every religious council and asked for the sponsorship of the Council of Hispanic Bishops, including the twenty-two bishops and their respective constituencies. We also visited each local council of ministers individually, as well as the ministerial associations, to clarify that they would not be breaking the law. Some asked why undocumented workers could not have come here legally, like other immigrants had. Others asked how they could reconcile support for the undocumented population with the strict moral code in our churches of respecting the law. So we taught them, preaching that the Bible said that when a law was unjust we should not submit to it (Acts 5:29). Indeed, we were responsible to a higher law.

When the day finally arrived, we gathered and marched across the Brooklyn Bridge to 26 Federal Plaza. Here I was with Senator Rubén Díaz and his son Rubén Díaz Jr. (now the Bronx borough president), leading the march alongside other prominent religious figures in our community. We marched and marched, and thousands and thousands arrived. Some media outlets estimated the crowd at 100,000. There was excitement and praise and chants. The people embraced the movement as something that was integral to their role as the people of God.

Indeed, people were still joining the rally hours later. Our religious community was there, as was the secular immigration-rights community. It also transcended ethnic groups. Asians, Haitians, and continental Africans were there. It became one of the city's most significant rallies. Without a doubt, we were resisting the established power represented by the political, religious, and media outlets in the city. The rally itself helped us build a momentum that facilitated the mobilization of our religious community to continue with the immigration reform issue.

After the rally, I received a call from Congressman Gutiérrez. He had just come off a rally in Chicago with a couple of thousand people. He had called it A Caravan of Hope for Immigration, and he wanted to hold a similar event in New York City. So he called NYS assemblyman José Rivera of the Bronx and asked him for a leader in the religious community. The assemblyman recommended me, and the congressman contacted me. I agreed to work with them and then convened a meeting of religious leaders.

We met with the elected officials and planned for a second rally, this time consisting mainly of the leadership. We had about a month to put it together, so we chose to hold it at La Sinagoga, a historical Pentecostal church in East Harlem on 125th Street, between Lexington and Park Avenues. Again, we went to the different factions, ministerial associations, bishops, and the radio stations. This time around, it was more difficult because we were dealing with the leadership and we had to navigate the egos involved.

We had to deal with who was going to sponsor and represent. Some people felt ignored, so I had to reassure them while I had to disassociate myself from others who had alienated the majority groups. We also invited immigration groups to co-sponsor the rally with us, but we made clear that it was going to be led by the church. We contacted elected officials and mobilized a significant number of the younger ministers. In the end, the rally was co-sponsored by LPAC, the Council of Hispanic Bishops, the New York Hispanic Clergy Association, and the Latino Leadership Circle. We also got free press from America's Voice, a Washington-based organization that deals with issues of immigration. We held a press conference with major TV stations in attendance.

Every elected official we could think of was in attendance. Almost three rows of seats were filled with city and state elected officials and party leaders. It was impressive. All three Latino NYC congressmen showed up. José Serrano, Nydia Velasquez (chair of the national Hispanic caucus), and Congressman Charlie Rangel attended. Even NYS Senator Charles Schumer showed up. The governor's office was represented by the Secretary of State, Lorraine Cortés-Vázquez. Also, our guest of honor, Congressman Gutiérrez, spoke. It truly was a powerful demonstration of the power of the church, as we were resisting the established power. Over two thousand church leaders attended.

A year later, we convened a meeting of the Latino Pentecostal evangelical leadership. This meeting was to be sponsored not only by the religious community but also by the immigrant organizations in New York. The religious organizations embraced my position that it was critical to work in coalition with the immigration civic groups, and vice versa. As a result, the event was convened by LPAC, New York Hispanic Clergy Association, Hispanic Bishops, the Latino Leadership Circle, Make the Road

New York, the Hispanic Federation, and the New York Immigration Co-alition. They all participated, and about seven hundred people attended the meeting at LPAC's headquarters in the Bronx, the Urban Ministry Complex. Again, Congressman Gutiérrez was the speaker of honor, and many other elected officials attended.

The rally itself was done in preparation for the March on Washington, and it allowed me to influence people to go to that rally. Indeed, even though President Obama said he supported immigration reform, we still confronted him in order to gain his official and active support.[1] We rented buses, and thousands of New Yorkers went with us to seek fair, systemic relief for immigrants. Nearly 200,000 others joined us from across the country. Since then, I have engaged U.S. Senators Charles Schumer and Hillary Clinton (now Secretary of State) to secure their support for immigration reform. As we related to these public officials, we were aware of the ongoing tension when interacting with the powers, even if they supported our cause. We knew that we had to exercise discernment even as we engaged them. Today, you may be the one to stand up for the least of these in society.

Provide a Prophetic Voice

The rally allowed me to emerge as a voice for immigration reform, within both the secular and religious communities. I was able to bring about considerable cooperation among the participating groups. I also built bridges between religious and community leaders and public officials. As in past experiences, I understood that I could be a prophetic voice to rally people around a cause, even if they were on opposite sides regarding other issues. The community's progress had to become the principal issue for everyone.

Regrettably, the church has not always provided a prophetic voice in response to the abuses by the powers. Too often, today's church has worshiped at the altar of materialism, consumerism, militarism, and state-sanctioned violence. It also has bought into and promoted images and

1. I believe our constant advocacy and meetings with the Obama Administration were part of the reason for President Obama's 2012 executive order, which effectively enabled the Dream Act. The executive order placed a two-year suspension on deportations of young people who were brought illegally to this country as children, and it provides the opportunity for them to apply for legal permanent residency.

messages that legitimize the powers' repressive edicts and policies. In too many ways, the church has linked its success to the benefits it could derive from the powers.

The silence by today's church has been motivated very much by a desire for acceptance and legitimacy. The church has found it difficult to be in but not of this world. Through the powers' leader — Satan (Isaiah 14:12) — the church at times has fallen for the oldest deception ever.

> Now the serpent was more crafty than any other beast of the field that the Lord God had made. He said to the woman, "Did God actually say, 'You shall not eat of any tree in the garden'?" (Genesis 3:1)

Satan prompted the original sin and has since tempted others to sin through deceptive acts (2 Corinthians 11:13-14). The church does not appear to have avoided this fate.

In its Sunday worship services, the church has tended to focus on personal piety rather than social justice, leaving mainly parachurch ministries to address and respond to the issues ravaging our society. In part, this is because, instead of being the underground voice that is unaccepted in the public square, the church now has a platform. It has chosen to be part of the majority culture and has rejected its original marginalized status. In our present reality, evangelicals and Pentecostals have arrived. They no longer are seen as "crazies." Now, they are at the political and cultural tables, so they tend to not push too much.

In many ways, the church has come to relate to the powers in a mainstream way. Gospel music has become a typical part of radio stations and awards shows. We even have our own music awards shows. Religious leaders have become political leaders. We have breakfast with the President of the United States. Our seminaries look like traditional universities, and at times employ traditional educational and corporate pedagogical models that reflect Wall Street more than the Jerusalem or Antioch models of the church. Even for our institutional symbols, we draw more from the corporate world and less from traditional Christianity. We also downplay the negative social impact of the powers' repressive laws and policies and unintentionally end up supporting and advancing them.

This is why Paul asks us to "be strong in the Lord and in the power of his might" (Ephesians 6:10). For this reason, he instructs us to prepare to face Satan and the power of the powers.

Therefore take up the whole armor of God, that you may be able to withstand in the evil day, and having done all, to stand firm. (6:13)

Thus, while the powers may try to point to policies and laws that are unfavorable to a given population or community but beneficial to the society at large, you should not see this as a substitute for a peaceful and just society. You need to be equipped with truth, righteousness, peace, faith, salvation, and the word of God. You also need to pray and plead for affected people and communities. In addition, you need to ensure that you can proclaim the gospel of Jesus Christ boldly (6:14-20).

This is why Paul also reminds us that we should not expect to carry out our call and struggle only in the earthly realm:

For we do not wrestle against flesh and blood, but against principalities, against powers, against the rulers of the darkness of this age, against spiritual hosts of wickedness in the heavenly places. (Ephesians 6:12)

Thus, while the powers may sometimes work on behalf of, and even bring about, concrete examples of peace and justice, you should not see the kingdom of man as a substitute for the Kingdom of God. It is very probable that the powers will use their vast assimilation apparatus to try to convince you that they act and speak for God. In fact, at times, their decrees may even mirror those of the Kingdom. However, you must recall the fallen nature of the powers and affirm your loyalty to the Kingdom of God. You also must agree to confront the powers when they fail to uphold Kingdom values for their citizens.

As the church has attempted to emulate the powers' systems and structures, it has rejected the Jerusalem church model, in which to each was given according to their need (Acts 2:45). It also has failed to challenge the monopoly of the powers. Certainly this trend reflects the ideology or belief systems of today's church. In reality, this dynamic has been a part of the church since its inception. To add insult to injury, the average church member has internalized, affirmed, and even perpetuated these belief systems. In effect, they have maintained the status quo, even when it has not always benefited the average citizen. This has allowed the powers to use the language of the church, which has facilitated their efforts to appear to be aligned to Kingdom values.

This is why the church must speak out in order to avoid being complicit toward the powers. This was the case with the apostles, who had to contend with the Roman establishment and the local Jewish Council, which had been installed by the Romans. After Pentecost, as the apostles were performing signs and wonders, they were gaining believers everywhere they went (Acts 5:12-14). At the same time, the Council, led by the Sadducees, rose against the apostles and put them in a public prison (5:17-18). Afterward, God brought about their release and instructed them to preach and teach in the temple (5:19-21).

Subsequently, the Council leaders took the apostles from the temple and set them before the Council. There, the high priest questioned them and reminded them of the order forbidding them from preaching the gospel of Jesus Christ.

> Did we not strictly command you not to teach in this name? And look, you have filled Jerusalem with your doctrine, and intend to bring this man's blood on us! (5:28)

But Peter and the apostles responded that "we must obey God rather than men" (5:29). Not surprisingly, this enraged the Council, who wanted to kill the apostles. But, after internal discussion, they just beat the apostles and released them, yet not before ordering them again not to speak in the name of Jesus (5:33-40). In turn, the apostles rejoiced that they suffered in the name of Jesus, and they continued to preach and teach daily the gospel of Jesus in the temple and from house to house (5:41-42).

WAR

This was my attitude when our country was in the shadow of the September 11 bombing of the World Trade Center. The United States was in the midst of heightened patriotic fervor, seemingly united around its opposition to what it perceived to be the new "evil empire" — a term that was basically code for the Muslim world. The political and religious powers, and public opinion, appeared to be in favor of a war against Iraq. The press was politically very conservative on the issue of war. At the time, there were few voices in print or on television criticizing it. Even the church embraced it almost as a holy crusade. The fundamentalist, evangelical wing of the church saw the war as the new rallying cry for organizing the "armies of God." In this environment, to be against the war had negative consequences.

This was the context for the invitation I received to give the invocation and speak at the first large demonstration against the Iraqi war in New York City. When I received a call from Father Paul Mayer, an activist Catholic priest I had known since the 1960s, to be the Pentecostal, Protestant, Latino voice in a religious coalition against the war, I was pleased because I already felt the war was not justified. In fact, I was one of the first Pentecostal evangelical Latino leaders to come out publicly against the war. I had no choice but to be a lone wolf, a maverick. There had been too many manipulations of the facts, I believed, and the circumstances did not rise to the level of a just war.

The time reminded me of my youth, when I had come out against the Vietnam War. It reminded me of the many young men who were brought home in body bags, and the division that it caused in this country. The situation in Iraq seemed to me like a civil war in which different religious and political factions were fighting to exercise political control. Just as with Vietnam, I believed that the church should stand up for peace rather than encourage war for reasons other than self-defense. I also knew that, in supporting the opposition to the war, I was resisting the established political, religious, and social powers.

As I sought advice as to whether I should attend the public demonstration, I consulted several elected officials who usually were progressive on these types of issues. Many actively discouraged me from such visible participation. They said it was too soon after September 11, and it could damage my standing and reputation in the community. I also asked religious leaders, and they certainly believed I would be stigmatized as a radical leftist who did not care for our country, which had been attacked without provocation. In the end, I respectfully disagreed and decided it was the right thing to participate in the event. Over fifty thousand people demonstrated that day against the war.

Ultimately, I was drawing on a long historical tradition in the church, which the powers within the religious community have tried to downplay. Instead, they have strived for accommodation or legitimization by the system and the status quo. But I was following the leading of the Spirit, regardless of what the established powers or the religious and community leaders were saying. I knew God would comfort me. He would give me peace in my soul. I knew he would vindicate me in time. In turn, his peace strengthened me to support other peace efforts and share our gospel mandate to be peacemakers. Today, you may be the one to champion peaceful responses in the Middle East, Africa, and other conflict-ridden regions.

POLICE BRUTALITY AND HOSTILITY

In the 1990s and 2000s, I became active around issues of police brutality and hostility in many of NYC's low-income communities of color. Anthony Baez, Amadou Diallo, Sean Bell: these names have been grafted into the community's collective consciousness. While the courts may have awarded significant financial restitution to these individuals or their families, they could not wipe out the emotional and physical wounds with which they, and the community, had been left behind to deal. In response, some community members wanted retribution. I went to the people and many came to me. I understood my task was to facilitate the community's desire to express its lament for unfavorable treatment.

In 2009 the courts awarded $7 million to the family of Sean Bell, who was killed by police officers during his bachelor party. The powers tried to focus on events that took place at Bell's bachelor party and lost the case. Some people wanted to capitalize on the public outcry surrounding this case. I agreed, but I knew we had to be strategic. We could not be seen as rabble rousers, as the powers always seem to target people like that. Rather, we needed to highlight the injustice while still reflecting the peace of God. We could not inadvertently bring about more violence while we were seeking an end to what many of us considered had become a police state in low-income communities of color.

Consequently, we petitioned to hold a public demonstration at 170th Street and Jerome Avenue in the Southwest Bronx, near LPAC's headquarters. The nearby 44th precinct was concerned at the outcry, fearing violence and confrontation. The police leadership met with me first, and then allowed us to stop traffic. Consistent with the image of iron and clay in Daniel's vision (Daniel 2), they were concerned about their public image. They realized we had public opinion on our side and that the press would portray them as antagonistic if they opposed us. Thus, the powers buckled under the pressure, and we held our demonstration. It hit the news, which lent more exposure to this issue. Today, you may be the one to highlight abuses by our law enforcement officers and the police hierarchy.

Ensure That Community Needs Are Met

Indeed, this is the nature and character of the powers. Unlike the forthcoming Kingdom of God, the powers do not seek to meet the needs of all their citizens, especially those who lack well-funded special interest groups to champion their causes. Without a doubt, the pharmaceutical lobby gets a quicker reception from the powers than an anti-poverty co-alition does. The powers can find billions to bail out the lending industry, while millions of average homeowners lose homes that often were al-ready out of their financial reach. While public officials shelter their cam-paign supporters, too many people have secured soon-to-be-defaulted government-sanctioned loans, which had fueled the myth that the Amer-ican Dream really was alive for them.

This dynamic reflects how fallen the powers are, even as they attempt to present themselves as responsive to the community's needs. In fact, you can be sure that, at some point, the powers will treat people unfavor-ably. The book of Acts helps us understand how to confront the powers while responding to the needs of the community. Here, Paul and Silas were in Philippi, a leading metropolitan area of Macedonia and a Roman colony. Philippi had well-established economic and political systems (Acts 16:12). On their way to a place of prayer, Paul and Silas encountered a slave girl who allegedly could tell fortunes (16:16-18). After several en-counters with the girl, Paul and Silas invoked the name of Jesus Christ and freed her of the spirit possessing her. Subsequently, the girl's owners seized Paul and Silas and dragged them to the marketplace, where they presented the two men to the local rulers (16:19).

To these businessmen, Paul and Silas had wrecked their economic as-set. They reasoned that Paul and Silas's act (of deliverance for the slave girl) was both alien and unlawful in relation to the laws of the powers (16:20-21). Those around them shouted in agreement with the girl's own-ers. Indeed, Paul and Silas had preached the gospel, which had negatively affected the economic system. Not surprisingly, the judges found them guilty and ordered them to be disciplined and incarcerated as per the pre-vailing legal practices. They also ordered the jailer to put Paul and Silas in the maximum security subdivision and keep them shackled (16:24).

In this context, Philippi's political, economic, and judicial systems were in cahoots, and average citizens were being treated as pawns. The political system protected the economic system, and the judicial system absorbed those who were deemed likely to disrupt the alliances and re-duce the anticipated profits. Average citizens were negatively impacted by this alliance, as evidenced by the political system not seeking to pro-tect the young woman. When Paul and Silas revealed the gospel, it shook up this status quo. In fact, their act revealed that the power of the gospel did not solely impact individuals (the slave girl), but also the treatment of people groups such as the poor, the marginalized, and the exploited. Indeed, their evangelistic deed had exposed the extent of Roman captivity. The result of personal freedom had systemic implications, which upset the systems and pushed them to mobilize to uphold their dominion.

Late that night, an act of God provided a means for Paul and Silas to be freed from their captivity; but they did not leave the prison. Instead, they trusted that God would deliver them from their captivity; they counted on God's intervention. They used the occasion to reveal Christ to the jailer, who, along with the rest of his household, was saved and subsequently baptized (16:27-33). The next morning, the judges released Paul and Silas, who then used the occasion to assert their citizenship and confront the unfair acts of the judicial system (16:35-37). In response, the judges apologized to them and released them, but asked them to leave the city quietly. Thus, by trusting God, they were released from jail and did not become fugitives. They left the city and visited Lydia, a recent convert, taking the time to encourage the local congregation in her house (16:39-40).

AFFORDABLE HOUSING

As a spiritual community leader, I have always been concerned about the needs of the community and have sought to ensure that the powers upheld their responsibility toward all their citizens. In the early 1970s, as the pastor of El Camino, I organized several community leaders to found the Sunset Park Redevelopment Corporation. The neighborhood of Sunset Park was in transition, with Puerto Ricans moving into a formerly white neighborhood, and there were tensions. Since I was already becoming well known in the local Pentecostal community, I was elected the first chairman. We all were part of the Puerto Rican community, which the white community had rejected for not fitting into what had been a middle-class white community.

Adding to the tensions was the fact that many newcomers had bought two-family homes, but were abandoning them due to mortgage foreclosures. This situation was part of the scandals in the 1970s of the Federal Housing Administration (FHA). Real estate agents were going to jail for having inflated buyers' salaries on paper in order to enable them to purchase homes that were in fact out of their price range. They had preyed on homeowners' aspirations and desires to live the American dream. On every block, homes were boarded up as they were being abandoned. Not surprisingly, the neighborhood began to deteriorate, which enraged the whites who remained.

In response to this crisis, we partnered with Lutheran Medical Center to take possession of these homes. Kathryn S. Wylde (now president and CEO of the Partnership for New York City) led Lutheran's local redevelopment efforts. We started buying the abandoned two-family homes from FHA and began to rehabilitate and sell them at a small profit to qualified homebuyers. Our goal was to stabilize the community by eliminating the eyesores that were contributing to the deterioration of the community. HUD owned the properties, but it resisted our plan. It had an enormous amount of red tape and put other obstacles in the way of our stabilizing the neighborhood. It argued that it could not sell houses at the low prices we wanted to pay. But we operated from the belief that the powers and their decrees were not invincible.

We held several meetings with HUD officials, but they failed to generate any momentum toward gaining access to the homes. Meanwhile, the community kept deteriorating, and some of the homes were being occupied by squatters, gang members, and drug dealers. After trying without success to negotiate with HUD, we determined that we had to confront them. With significant community support, we resisted HUD's decrees, organized, and took over 26 Federal Plaza. For this direct action, I had met with members of the community, particularly The Way Pentecostal Rehabilitation Center, a residential facility we had birthed for the rehabilitation of drug addicts and alcoholics. Along with several of its residents, members of my congregation, and other community-based groups, over sixty community residents demonstrated in front of 26 Federal Plaza.

We were at the strongman's house, believing that God would make a way. We threatened to stay until HUD changed the policy to enable us to rehabilitate the foreclosed homes and thus strengthen and stabilize our community. In a very intense meeting with the HUD regional head, we demanded that HUD turn over the homes to the Corporation. A few days later, HUD did so. Afterward, we rehabilitated and sold the homes, which resulted in the revitalization of the community. God had intervened. Today, you may be the one to ensure that the powers provide affordable services and resources to the community.

PUBLIC EDUCATION

During this same time, I also was director of both the United Puerto Rican Organization of Sunset Park (UPROSE) and the Neighborhood Manpower Center. These roles involved me in educational reform, job development, poverty, welfare rights, and other issues. We also were in the midst of the great struggle for community control of public education. I remember a young teacher, Carmen Perez, who later became a statewide leader in bilingual education. She was threatened, intimidated, and called all kinds of names for taking a stand on behalf of children who were consistently failing. Indeed, her decision to cross the picket line caused division and polarization among her own ranks. But she was faithful, and her courage inspired me to continue in the struggle.

The city was divided. There was anger, hostility, suspicion, and distrust among the different groups involved in the struggle. The teachers' union, the United Federation of Teachers (UFT), was pitted against parent and community groups. The black and Puerto Rican communities were against the white community. Charges of racism and anti-Semitism ran rampant on both sides. Eventually, the UFT held a strike, which paralyzed and polarized the NYC public schools. This led to the Board of Education closing every public school. With the support of brave teachers who crossed the picket lines, I helped community and parent groups reopen them as freedom schools.

There I was, confronting the system in the midst of racial and ethnic turmoil. But I felt strangely at ease. I felt the shalom of God. As Paul promised, I was enveloped by the peace of God, which surpasses all understanding. It guarded my heart and mind in Christ Jesus. I felt justice was on my side; the system was wrong. Black and Puerto Rican children should have good schools. They should have the same opportunities as white children. We were a community in captivity, and Moses' "Let my people go!" message to the Egyptians resonated with me. I had said yes to serve as God's messenger!

In the late 1980s, I became a parent organizer around issues of quality education in East Harlem and the Lower East Side. Already, data showed a direct relationship between school grades and incarceration rates and a whole group of sociological problems that ultimately would destroy the children of that school district. Thus I empowered parents to change the school system that had underserved their children and failed to treat them with the attention, respect, and dignity they deserved.

At this time, we were dealing with the decentralization of schools, school board elections, and the hiring of minority principals and super-intendents. It was a time of nationalistic sentiment, in which we wanted to see some of our own in positions of influence and power. Through these efforts, many Hispanics and African Americans were elected to the school boards, and many were appointed and elected to principalships and assistant principalships. In the Lower East Side, our organizing efforts resulted in the naming of a Puerto Rican superintendent of the local school district, after twenty years of Puerto Ricans not having been represented in the leadership of the superintendent's office.

While we made some progress and we realized some shifts in the achievement levels for children of color, the progress was not long-lasting. Ethnic tensions, both within and outside our own constituencies, began to emerge. While there was vision and idealism and a sense that we needed to do better for our children, we did not transcend our own individual situations. We also did not discern that our struggles to reform the educational system had not only a personal dimension but also a systemic one. It had to do not only with transforming the systems, but also with transforming ourselves. Eventually, the factionalism within our own community reappeared. It led to schisms and ultimately to the defeat of this reform movement.

As I organized parents, the powers greatly resisted. They made many attempts to stop me, including character assassination, bureaucratic control, spreading rumors, and creating suspicion within the teachers and administrators in the district. They even took letters I would sign "In Peace and Freedom," and twisted that closing to imply that I was a member of a revolutionary, terrorist Puerto Rican organization, which supposedly used that phrase as its signature. They charged that I was really trying to create revolution and destroy the school system, and even incite parents to commit violent acts. This accusation could not have been further from reality.

"In Peace and Freedom" simply came from my Christian ministry background. It stood for the peace of God and the freedom we have in God through Christ. I saw these attacks by the powers of the school board and the school bureaucracy as perpetrated by evil spirits, the roaring lion that was influencing the principalities and powers. I was discouraged, as I was trying to organize parents to seek out justice for their children. I knew these tactics were designed to make me leave the battlefield. But I resisted the powers and the traps set for me. Ultimately, I was able to navigate and resist the powers. Today, you may be the one to speak out for improved public education for all children.

Oppose Efforts to Indoctrinate the Community

Without a doubt, the powers will do everything to neutralize those who confront them. One strategy they employ is to indoctrinate people into their secular worldview, which seeks to negate the absolute authority of God and his kingdom. In my ministry, I have always emphasized that the Kingdom of God is supreme over all kingdoms (Psalm 103:19; 145:11-13). Of course, the powers do not accept the power and dominion of God and his Kingdom.

Instead, they advance secularism, which emphasizes a relativism that leads to the questioning and rejection of all moral constraints. "If it feels good, do it!" becomes the cry of the society. Selfishness, arrogance, pride, rebellion: these approaches to life become the building blocks of this "me" lifestyle. Yet I submit that this is just idolatry masquerading under a new name.

Leading the charge in favor of this lifestyle are fallen and abusive institutions that are working tirelessly to indoctrinate people to this self-centered way of life. In many respects, these political, economic, and social institutions control the content of our everyday conversations, and they convince many people of their merits. Too often, this has kept many from confronting the faithless, secular powers — the kingdom of man. Indeed, the Apostle Paul reveals who is behind these reprehensible efforts:

> In their case the god of this world has blinded the minds of the unbelievers, to keep them from seeing the light of the gospel of the glory of Christ, who is the image of God. (2 Corinthians 4:4, NRSV)

Too often, the church has failed to discern the corporate manifestations of Satan. In fact, Satan works through the powers, exercising dominion and rule through laws and deep-set traditions. Often, the powers are strengthened by his efforts. Nevertheless, Christ shows us how to resist. When Satan tempted him, Jesus resisted his corruption (Matthew 4:8-10). In the process, he showed the limits of Satan (Job 1:12; 2:6). Ultimately, Satan's influence will end (Revelation 12:9-10). John calls us to test every spirit in order to ensure we do not follow the spirit of the antichrist, which is among us. This way, we also can distinguish between the Spirit of truth and the spirit of error (1 John 4:1-6).

Of course, when interacting with the power's systems and structures, the possibility always exists for them to attempt to co-opt and limit you. This is the case especially if you have a prophetic voice. Not surprisingly, you have to disconnect from these efforts, which can be difficult. In my case, I did not always know that I had to disengage until challenges arose. I had resolved to give the powers the benefit of the doubt as the potential was there to make a meaningful impact. Like Joseph and Mordecai, I also wanted to bring about pro-community laws and public policies. But it became clear that the powers were maintaining seemingly positive relationships with my community and me, while they also perpetrated negative actions toward us.

UNITED NATIONS (SPIRITUAL REVOLUTION DAY)

At times, I took the initiative to remind my community that it should be loyal to God and not to the powers. During the peace movement of the early 1970s, I would wonder why hippies were the ones who got all the press concerning peace. To me, Christ is the Prince of Peace, and I wanted the world to recognize this truth. So two ministers I knew, Rev. Wilfredo Laboy and Rev. Benjamin Alicea, helped me organize a peace rally, which we called "Spiritual Revolution Day at the United Nations: Proclaiming Jesus Christ as the Prince of Peace." For this, we mobilized youth councils of Pentecostal groups. We created a logo of the cross and a fist, in solidarity with the Black Power movement.

Initially, the Assemblies of God, Spanish Eastern District, boycotted the rally, largely because of our logo. However, I met with Superintendent Rev. Adolfo Carrion Sr., who agreed to allow the youth councils to participate. With the youth on board, we worked to gain media attention. The Thursday before the rally, a core group of forty youth leaders went to take over the U.N. chapel for Christ. We established a division of labor, in which we separated general members from those who would confront the powers. We understood that not everyone had to go beyond the acceptable norms. Only a select few would participate at the next level. Still, both sectors understood their unique role in the struggle to be openly militant for the Lord.

"Christ is the real Prince of Peace!" served as our rallying cry. With Bibles in our coats, we entered slowly into the chapel. People were inside the chapel and we told them that we were taking the chapel over in the name of Christ. We let the people leave. When U.N. security came to ask who was in charge, we said that Jesus was our leader. Then, just before the U.N. closed for the day, we walked out and talked to the press. That Saturday, four to five thousand young people came to the rally. The news media were there, too, reporting on our action.

NYC BOARD OF EDUCATION (PS64 ANNEX)

In the late 1990s, I had to respond differently in a partnership with Public School 64, a school near LPAC's Urban Ministry Complex. At the time, I was confronting the NYC Department of Education to achieve quality education for students in Bronx School District Nine, the city's lowest performing school district. I established an annex for PS 64, in which we provided the physical space and had input into the management and culture of the school. We also had a joint committee consisting of members of LPAC and PS 64, which interviewed and recommended the school personnel, because I wanted to show that our children could learn.

After a few years, I felt that we were not equals because of all of the legal red tape and the bureaucracy in the Board of Education. School officials had final approval of all teachers, the coordinator, curriculum, rules and regulations, and space allocation. We just had input. This inequality became real when we tried to get a teacher-assigned coordinator and experienced great resistance. The school officials wanted us to be a landlord, not a partner. Yet our original purpose had been to create an alternative mini-school that would have a different culture and a high level of educational excellence.

Because PS 64 was a failing school, we wanted to have joint power to choose effective leaders. The school officials came back, citing Board of Education rules and laws that non-Board of Education people could not be involved officially in the decision-making process. We finally reached consensus that, while it would not be official, we would be participants and partners in this process. This was all on the word of the principal, who supported this type of relationship. But officially, it had no standing. As a result, we were not able to make the kind of impact we sought for the children of our community. Indeed, this reality moved me to establish the Family Life Academy Charter School.

As I confronted the powers, I tackled issues that dealt with the oppression and marginalization of the communities in which I ministered. I went directly to the centers of power and denounced their actions and policies, crying out against their injustices. Sometimes, the powers accused me of being divisive and speaking only for myself. Other times, they tried to silence me through arrests and by belittling our positions. But I stood firm. I spoke truth to power. I held them accountable. I also included other voices in these efforts. In the end, the powers adopted some policies that reflected Kingdom values. They also relented at times when facing community pressure. They succumbed to God's forces. I hope my efforts help you envision ways that God may be calling you to confront the powers.

CHAPTER 8

A Few Things to Consider
as You Minister in Captivity

⌒⁂⌒

S o, are you excited to engage and confront your community? What about the powers? Even after forty-five years, I keep asking the Lord to give me more years to minister in all four ways. As you may have noticed, each way to minister in captivity asks you to adopt and apply a particular strategy in order to be consistent with your historical context and with God's transcendent vision for his creation. At the same time, there are further considerations that can inform and guide you in ministering in captivity, whether you minister in one or in all four ways.

As you carry out your ministry, I ask you to consider the following counsel:

- Don't be conformed to this world
- Don't throw out the church with the bath water
- Embrace the new movements of God

Incorporating these truths into my ministry has been valuable. I believe they will also help you as you minister in captivity. In this case, one size does fit all!

Don't Be Conformed to This World

In a sense, this book has been all about not conforming to this world. Still, I find it too important a point not to say it explicitly. Throughout

my life, some people have criticized me for my supposedly nonconform-
ist ways, as if I were fighting against the powers and their systems and
structures randomly, or for its own sake. Yet I wonder how such individuals would want me to act instead. Would they prefer that I was a rugged
individual? Follow the crowd blindly? Paint a rosy picture and overlook
the thorns? Advance society's agenda in spite of my Kingdom values?
Turn a blind eye to injustice and conflict? Trust conventional wisdom before the wisdom of God? In my spirit, I cannot see myself doing any of
these things. Over and over, I have found myself citing Peter and the
apostles in Acts 5:29, when they were before the ruling party: "We must
obey God rather than any human authority" (NRSV). I have not known
any other way, so I can suggest no other way.

And yes, I have received more criticism than I may have desired or
thought I deserved. I have lost friends, supporters, and potential funders.
But many others have responded to my clarity of vision, sense of purpose, and service to God's people and to society in general. Such people
are in the highways and byways. They also are inside the palace and at the
King's gate, speaking for and leading people to righteous living and peace
and justice. Like me, they may appear to be on the margins, but they represent the heartbeat of the Kingdom of God. Our citizenship in this
Kingdom requires that we be different in this world, even if it means others consider us controversial. All I can say is that, in the end, God's faithfulness will enable you to persevere even when you face trials. He also
blesses you with traveling companions, family and friends, who make
your ministry life a joy. Let me share with you some key ideas that have
helped me not to conform.

Accept That You Are Part of the Collective, and Not Just an Individual

As Christians, we are part of a covenant or contract with God, which
gives us a different worldview. This covenant calls us to a transcendent
life that is non-materialistic and non–consumer oriented. It is aligned
with spiritual values that do not conform to this world. In both the old
and new covenants, God asked his people to disconnect from the materi-
alistic, carnal values of this world. One of those worldly values is the idea
that we are just individuals.

On one level, this seems obvious. Yet individualism is the dominant
view in our country. It is rooted in ideas about rugged self-reliance and

personal responsibility. It implies that you should be able to pull yourself up by your bootstraps, and that you have the power to overcome every difficulty alone. The next time you're in a large bookstore, stop and look at how many books are geared toward personal development and self-esteem. In many ways, everything is reduced to or focuses on empowering the individual. The view stresses that the individual should be able to navigate and transcend all the situations that are impacting him or her.

This view of the power of the individual is being fed to us through every means of communication — both implicitly and explicitly, both officially and unofficially. From a political perspective, its supporters point to the U.S. Declaration of Independence, which affirms that we, as individuals, are endowed with certain unalienable rights and that we must fight for these rights individually. We also hear it in the language of the popular culture: *I have rights. No one can violate my rights. I'm first.* This seems to be what is important. But is it true? As we examine this notion of individualism more closely, I submit that we are not just individuals.

The closer we look, the more we see that we are part of a collective, a community, a family. We are more than the sum total of individuals. We are part of a collective expression. We are the sum total of everything that has happened to us. The past has had an impact on us. Our present circumstances impact us. Even our anxiety and worry about the future has an impact on us. As part of the collective, we are informed by a collective unconscious.[1] As the Bible puts it, it is the great cloud of witnesses (Hebrews 12:1), which surrounds us and impacts us, directly and indirectly. We may not be clear exactly who influenced our thoughts or actions, but we acknowledge that they came from others who lived before us.

Indeed, the concept of a collective is well established in the Bible. Yes, God created Adam. But then he created Eve, and they became a community. He is the God of Abraham, Isaac, and Jacob. He is the God of the twelve tribes of Israel. He also is the head of the body of Christ. When he called Abraham, he said, "I will bless you and make you a great name. In you all the families of the earth shall be blessed" (12:2-3). In the Ten Commandments which he gave to Moses, the first five deal with humanity's relationship to God. But the next five deal with human beings and their

1. Carl Jung also addresses the collective unconscious from a psychoanalytical perspective in his *The Archetypes and the Collective Unconscious* (London: Routledge, 1996) and *Man and His Symbols* (Garden City, NY: Doubleday, 1964).

relationships to each other, and what they should do or not do to one another. Community and social responsibility have been fundamental to God's plan for his creation from the beginning.

So I reiterate with a tremendous sense of authority, grounded both in Scripture and in my life experience. We are not only individuals. We are members of a collective. This reality informed me in the 1960s when I joined the NYC Council Against Poverty and started the NYC Puerto Rican Council Against Poverty. In the 1970s it prompted me to found Acción Cívica Evangélica and the Hispanic Council of the Reformed Church in America. In the 1980s it helped me work for Assemblyman Del Toro, while still confronting systemic sin and involving my community. In the 1990s and beyond, it has informed my work building partnerships and collaborations and sharing resourcing through the Latino Pastoral Action Center.

Be Mindful Not to Advance the Kingdom of Man's Agenda

The systems of the world will come at you in subtle ways. They will try to mold you through subliminal messages and strategies to conform you to the patterns of this world. They will rarely be so blatant and bold as to directly ask you to commit adultery or steal from the poor. Instead, acts of injustice will take on the appearance of legitimacy. They will be wrapped up in the language of rugged individualism, which has been the philosophy of the so-called "Me Generation": *Take care of yourself first. If it feels good, do it.* This conformity promises illumination and understanding. But it is rooted in self-centeredness.

I remember when the powers would manipulate communities into fighting for crumbs. By withholding all but the most basic resources, they were certain that we would not raise our voices against their divisive policies and would concentrate on infighting. Yet over time, as I gained public recognition for some of my work, I used that platform to advance the Kingdom. I had received recognition for my stances and actions, so they had to hear more of my views and my call to action in my acceptance speeches. Like Mordecai, I was going back to the king's gate (Esther 6:12). I took those opportunities to remind public officials and others that our work was far from done.

I will forever be inspired by Carmen Perez, who was a young teacher when I met her in the 1980s and later became a statewide leader in bilingual education. Even after she was threatened, intimidated, and called all kinds of horrific names, she took a stand on behalf of public school children. During a teachers' strike she crossed the picket line, which caused division and polarization among her own ranks. But she did not let herself be molded by the competing efforts of two worldly powers, the Board of Education and the United Federation of Teachers. She advanced a Kingdom agenda, even when it was extremely difficult.

We should not forget that this push to be conformed to this world has a mind behind it. It has an author, and he is a liar and a master deceiver. Paul puts it this way:

> You once walked according to the course of this world, according to the prince of the power of the air, the spirit who now works in the sons of disobedience, among whom also we all once conducted ourselves in the lusts of our flesh, fulfilling the desires of the flesh and of the mind, and were by nature children of wrath, just as the others. (Ephesians 2:2-3)

Too often we underestimate the power of Satan and of the fallen systems and structures. We take their power and ability to conform us to their thinking and actions too lightly. The truth is that we are not free, independent thinkers whose wisdom comes from our own personal well of knowledge. We do not make decisions in a vacuum. In reality, our views often reflect the mind-set of these fallen collective connections. Their power to mold and squeeze us into their way of thinking is sometimes insurmountable.

Think of the many "good," "decent" men and women in the world who have lived in societies that commit atrocities like slavery or genocide, sometimes even in the name of God. Or, for a less extreme example, remember that elder in Holland, Michigan. He seemed to have an admirable degree of personal piety, but he had also internalized the dominant culture's dehumanizing stereotypes of Latinos.[2] The most righteous individuals in the world are not immune to groupthink.

For this reason, you should never forget that all human systems are

---

2. Reinhold Niebuhr addresses the brutality and dehumanization of our society in his *Moral Man and Immoral Society: A Study of Ethics and Politics* (Louisville: Westminster John Knox Press, 2002) and *Christ and Culture* (New York: Harper, 1956). More recently, Stanley Hauerwas addresses this point among evangelicals in his book *The Peaceable Kingdom: A Primer in Christian Ethics* (Notre Dame, IN: University of Notre Dame Press, 1991).

fallen. They all have been affected by the Fall. They are sinful. They miss the mark. The wisdom they have birthed and facilitated is fallen. Their policies and practices tend to move us away from God and toward self-centeredness, toward being our own little gods. For some reason, we accept them as basically good, and thus look to them for direction and as our value system. It is not that these systems do not have any positive aspects at all or have never done any good. But we cannot forget their captive state.

Unfortunately, captive systems can sometimes take on the aura of the Kingdom of God. For example, when the economy surged in the 1990s, the church blessed the status quo because supposedly anyone could live the American dream of owning a home and a car. So the church effectively baptized the culture as tantamount to the Kingdom of God. However, when our economic system failed in the 2000s, many thousands of people lost their homes and other worldly possessions. Of course, many were never really able to afford these luxuries in the first place and had borrowed heavily to finance them.

Across the country, vast tracts of formerly thriving neighborhoods lay abandoned or empty, with remaining residents weathering the shame and decay that comes from living in a declining community. It was now obvious that fallen human policies and strategies, not divine handiwork, had led to these illusory dreams. Individuals and banks had sought personal riches, not true social prosperity. As you minister in captivity, you must be vigilant in discerning when you unwittingly are advancing human policies and when you are truly aligning the world around you to the values of the Kingdom of God.

Reject Conventional Wisdom When Not Aligned with Kingdom Values

Of course, the fallen systems are not the only ones that attempt to move us away from trusting God. At times, the people around us urge us to follow conventional wisdom that is not really aligned with Kingdom values. Too often, I have encountered well-intentioned individuals who were primarily concerned with the relative comfort they gained through their obedience to conventional wisdom. Comfort can be appealing, but Kingdom values are sure to bring about discomfort and even outright conflict in the society.

Had I accepted conventional wisdom, NYTS never would have established the seminary-undergraduate program with Adelphi University and funding from the Lilly Endowment in 1973. I would have joined the ranks of Iraqi War supporters after the national tragedy on September 11, 2001. FLACS would not have become a model for working with English language learners. We would not have contributed to increased opportunities for unapologetically evangelical churches and ministries that sought public funds. Conventional wisdom would have had me compromise our "extreme" agenda in order to receive government funding. But Kingdom wisdom would never allow such a thing.

Don't Throw Out the Church with the Bath Water

I will be the first to tell you that I have not always had the support of my religious community. At times, I have had to go to great lengths to get them to embrace both the personal and the social dimensions of their faith, let alone adopt and apply a holistic ministry paradigm. Like Paul, I have also had to deal with opponents within the church who spoke negatively about me and my ministries. Yet I understood that my responsibility was to be faithful to the Lord. I knew that the church could at times be an obstacle to the work of the Kingdom of God. But the church is still the body of Christ, and he is returning for her (Revelation 19:7). Who is going to help her be ready for his return?

Regrettably, the church has to account for some lamentable behavior. The history books and the public record have no problem pointing out her many failures. At the same time, the church has done immense good; yet you will find less public praise for the positive things the church has done over the centuries. The Christian backgrounds of historical events and leaders have been deemphasized. You have probably heard Martin Luther King Jr. referred to as "Dr. King." But when was the last time you heard him referred to as "*Rev.* Dr. King"? To think that the son of a pastor, who was a pastor himself, would have his pastoral credentials completely deemphasized! Similarly, people know Cesar Chavez as a community/union organizer, but how many know that his motivation came from his spirituality? He always saw his mission as a spiritual calling. What would Rev. Dr. Martin Luther King Jr. say to that? What would Cesar Chavez say?

I will not tell you that every relationship I have had with God's people has been fruitful. But I have tried to love my neighbor, including those who have considered me an enemy. Let me share with you some thoughts about connecting to God's people.

Acknowledge That the Church Has Both Hurt and Helped Society

While you minister in captivity, don't be surprised that some will charge the church with having selective amnesia. In many ways, the church has sanitized its history, presenting itself as the epitome of morality and exemplary conduct. For example, the evangelical Pentecostal church thinks of itself as proudly pro-life because it champions the rights of the unborn. Yet it also advocates for the death penalty and pro-death policies. Likewise, in moments of its history, the church has been in the vanguard of support for racial purity and apartheid policies. It has argued for segregation and against interracial marriage. These attitudes and deeds can still be seen in some religious communities today.

Regrettably, the more conservative side of the white evangelical church pretty much sat out of the civil rights movement. Indeed, at times you would have found the church on the other side of this movement, championing the status quo of racial separation. Today, you can often see the same thing with the women's movement and with reform movements in the areas of labor and environmentalism. Those of us who are loyal to the church that proclaims personal transformation in Christ would do well to confess and apologize for these acts that we have helped to perpetuate. We need to face them head on and repent.

The behavior of the church on these and other issues has served as a stumbling block and obstacle for many people who might otherwise embrace the message of personal transformation in Christ. It behooves us to clarify unequivocally that such behavior is contrary to the liberating message of our Lord and Savior Jesus Christ. Make no mistake about it! There is a difference between the organized church and Christ — the head of the body of Christ. I am not saying that Christ is not present in or leader of the organized church. But he certainly does not endorse any of the church's acts that advance the kingdom of man's values.

You can see this in Revelation 2–3, in which Christ calls out the churches in Asia Minor for behaving contrary to the mission he gave his church. For example, the church in Ephesus abandoned its first love, having moved away from practicing its initial godly ministry. The church in Pergamum dwelt where Satan's throne was, which had become a stumbling block to its members. The church in Thyatira had Jezebel, who was unduly influencing its members.

At the same time, Christ affirms that these churches still are part of his body. He embraces Ephesus for its doctrinal vision and its endurance.

He praises Pergamum for holding fast to Christ's name and not denying the faith. He notes how Thyatira showed its growing love through deeds of service. So you can see that Christ is present in the churches, even as he rebukes them for doing ministry in a way inconsistent with his liberating message. This is a paradox or creative tension that the church lives with daily.

Thankfully, the church also has been faithful to Christ's mission throughout history. It has created hospitals, schools, universities, and community programs. It has been a leader in disaster relief. It has helped millions of people become productive citizens and overcome addiction to drugs and alcohol. It has helped restore marriages. It has brought people into active participation in its life, sometimes even into leadership roles. It has helped people become civically engaged and to become business leaders and community leaders. It has helped people engage in politics and even run for office, pushing for passage of policies that promote Kingdom values. The fruit of their engagement has led to desegregation, women's suffrage, fair labor relations and practices, and civil and human rights, among others.

So as you can see, the church has perpetuated atrocities but it has also served as a catalyst for positive change in society. *Because of these atrocities, you might hear people say, I'm not going to be part of the church. I can't see myself as a member. I can't defend the institutional church.* You can tell these people that they should not only look at the negative actions of the church. They must also look at the positive contributions of the church.

This is why I have always been conscious of the paradox or creative tension within the church and its institutions. But I have always chosen to see treasures in earthen vessels. I have tried to recognize that, while the Lutheran Medical Center had excluded Hispanic clergy until I helped create the pilot CPE program for Hispanics, it also was providing affordable health care for the broader Hispanic and poor community. It even developed innovative family health centers that afforded the community residents primary care physicians, which was not common at the time. At New York Theological Seminary, while programs were not being offered to poor Hispanics, particularly the emerging Pentecostal community, until I helped bring about the college-seminary partnership that opened the doors to this growing population, the seminary had opened its doors to African Americans and had become a hub for inner-city practitioners who wanted to minister to the urban poor.

Resist Joining Critics Inside and Outside the Church

This is why we should not simply join the naysayers in the church and the critics who put down the church. We should be able to discern and highlight those times when the church has been light and salt in the world. Skeptical individuals may focus on the inconsistencies in the Bible and point to the early apostolic church as being inconsistent and full of division. They may say that the apostles endorsed racism and sexism and justified the accumulation of wealth. They may point out that the Bible reinforces the superiority of men and subordinates women. They may refer to God's endorsement of war. However, all these arguments stem from a superficial, non-holistic reading of the Scriptures. When we read the Bible carefully and take it as a whole, we see that these skeptical opinions have no basis.

Indeed, the truth of the matter is that the Scriptures never argue that the church is perfect. The Bible openly reveals the church's contradictions. When you read the Bible, you get to see people in all their imperfections. You see polygamy, incest, rape, violence, adultery, murder, and so on. The Bible never attempts to sanitize or distance itself from the human condition and the consequences of the Fall and captivity. James does not hide the classism and the lack of care for the poor within the church:

> Listen, my beloved brethren: Has God not chosen the poor of this world to be rich in faith and heirs of the kingdom which He promised to those who love Him? But you have dishonored the poor man. Do not the rich oppress you and drag you into the courts? Do they not blaspheme that noble name by which you are called? (James 2:5-7)

At the same time, he provides answers to help these wayward believers return to godly ways (4:1-12).

For his part, Paul is forthright about the nebulous spirituality that some of the churches had adopted, and about how some factions within them were attempting to hijack the concept of grace. He does not hide the reality that there were division, schisms, and outright animosity between church members: "For you are still carnal. For where there are envy, strife, and divisions among you, are you not carnal and behaving like mere men?" (1 Corinthians 3:3). The Bible is transparent about the church's imperfections. Thus, you can declare unapologetically why our captive world needs Christ's liberating message of holistic ministry. And you can declare that no one is required to live a perfect, sinless life in order to be an instrument of God's liberating activity in the midst of captivity. Indeed, God works through our human frailty.

Embolden the Church to Employ Its Resources to Advance Kingdom Values

So just how do you become an instrument of God's liberating activity? In my own life, I have utilized spiritual disciplines to advance Kingdom values.[3] I have never been able to bring the church around to a Kingdom perspective without a great deal of prayer, meditation, and reflection. These disciplines have empowered me to be dependent on God's Spirit in discerning my call and the role I have had to play both in the church and in the community. Indeed, God not only calls, but he guides and directs us.

It is these spiritual disciplines that will give you the strength to stand firm as you engage and confront your community and the powers. Be assured that God will sustain you as you uphold your Kingdom values, even in demanding and challenging situations. Think of the abolition of slavery, the Great Awakenings, women's suffrage, labor rights, civil rights, immigrant rights. These issues have affected millions of people and required God's people to rely on a source greater than themselves. They needed God's strength and comfort.

In the Scriptures, we see Isaiah receiving his vision from God and subsequently praying and confessing his sins. In the midst of that experience, he discerned and accepted God's call on his life. We see the prophetess Anna in the temple, a senior citizen and widow, waiting on the fulfillment of the promised Messiah, who would deliver God's people from oppression. She worshiped, fasted, and prayed day and night until Christ's arrival at the temple (Luke 2:36-40). Moses and Jesus held forty-day fasts. Paul fasted for three days in solitude after his encounter with the resurrected Jesus on the road to Damascus (Acts 9:9). Certainly John the Baptist cultivated the discipline of simplicity as a lifestyle. In these and many other instances, the spiritual disciplines empowered them to stand firm in the midst of their challenging and even overwhelming circumstances.

---

3. Although not exhaustively, Richard Foster makes the connection between the spiritual disciplines and social action/justice in *A Celebration of Discipline: The Path to Spiritual Growth* (New York: HarperCollins, 2002).

You also can learn about the strengths and weaknesses of the church and integrate them into your practice of holistic ministry. As I already stated, the church has both hurt and helped the society. You can never assume that others know this to the degree they should. Depending on the wing of the church they belong to, they have either minimized or denied the work of the church, or else have romanticized or overemphasized its contributions. This is why you need to develop a balanced, integrated approach that will educate and equip both you and others with a new way of looking at the church. You could lead a Bible study that looks at the Word of God from this perspective, showing the church as imperfect, but also as a place of refuge, renewal, and regeneration.

Yet another way is by developing a holistic ministry method that enables you to address the personal and social dimensions of your faith. If you remember God's creative process during the first six days of creation, you recall that he assessed, planned, implemented, and evaluated (Genesis 1:2-4a). I call this the "APIE Method." This process teaches us to work, or serve, even in the midst of darkness and chaos. We learn to build on God's foundations so that we may reflect his goodness. Of course, while these steps appear to be linear in order, they tend to overlap and may even require you to go back and forth. Thus, the creative process is ongoing and dynamic.

Let's say that you have always dreamed of being a teacher but lacked a high school diploma. You want to make this dream a reality, so you plan or prepare to take the necessary steps to become a certified teacher. You get your GED, complete college, and even go to graduate school. You implement or carry out each step of your plan, even if you are delayed or interrupted at times. Maybe you have to take a semester off to work, or maybe you can only go to school part-time because you have to raise your children. But you stay focused on your goal by keeping close to God and your community of support. In your final evaluation or review, I would expect to hear that you were hired at a school, maybe even our Family Life Academy Charter School. In this role, you would enable your students to become highly literate, critical thinkers, contributors to their families and communities, and concerned about and active around the socioeconomic, political, and even spiritual issues facing the society.

The same process holds true on an institutional level. Let's say you have assessed that your community lacks quality schools. Next, you would plan to challenge a group of individuals from your church and the community to develop a locally controlled public school. Then you would organize your church or faith-based community ministry to implement your plan. This would include petitioning the authorizing agencies, developing a school plan and curriculum, securing space, hiring personnel, and establishing collaborations with related support services and institutions. In your evaluation, I would expect to hear that the school is thriving, with the children meeting or surpassing the standards, teachers functioning at the highest professional levels, and the parents and communities actively involved in the life of the school.

A final way is to prepare people to be light and salt by assuming leadership roles in the public square. This would be the way to take your ministry outside of the four walls of the church to advance Kingdom values. Thus, they could serve as leaders in PTAs, community planning boards, school boards, block associations, social service agencies, and community-based organizations. They may even hold elected and appointed positions in the government. This would mean developing and using the church's internal teaching ministries to empower your people for these leadership roles.

Embrace the New Movements of God

Thankfully, God has continued to work in the church to prepare it for its mission. Indeed, God has not left his people on their own (Psalm 139:13-14; Acts 17:24-26). In fact, the Scriptures reveal that God is involved in his creation at all levels, having initiated each era of human history. His involvement stems from his promise to bless *all* nations through Abraham (Genesis 12:1-10). His promised new covenant came after he had a long, intimate relationship with his people.

> "Behold, the days are coming," says the Lord, "when I will make a new covenant with the house of Israel and with the house of Judah — not according to the covenant that I made with their fathers in the day that I took them by the hand to lead them out of the land of Egypt, my covenant which they broke, though I was a husband to them," says the Lord. (Jeremiah 31:31-32)

In Jesus, God would come in the flesh to be with his people. Later, the Holy Spirit would move us beyond our cultural and religious boundaries to bless all humankind.

Indeed, we need to embrace the new movements of God. Throughout human history, God has produced divine connections in people's lives to help them fulfill his plan and purpose (Genesis 24; 29:15–30:34; 1 Kings 19:15-22; John 1:41-42; Acts 13; 16:1-5). He has brought about divine appointments or meetings (Acts 3:1-10; 3:11-26; 16:11-15). At times, he has made divine interruptions in order to realize his own plans (John 21:1-19; Acts 9:1-9). Other times, he has caused divine delays due to our lack of faith in his power (Numbers 14:26-35).

I can testify to God's movement in my life and the world around me. Over the course of my life I have been awed by his concern for ordinary people and situations. Barren women have birthed children. Sick people have become healthy. Failing marriages have been restored. Depressed communities are now thriving. As I have felt his ongoing presence, I have learned some things I now share with you.

Accept God's Dynamic Activity in History Rather Than the Status Quo

God's will is intertwined with human history. He is not a static God. He is a moving God, who moves in the different situations that humanity experiences. He moves across time, too, calling each new generation of believers in new ways. Yet some have resisted and reacted; some have clung to former ways. They have not discerned the new things God is doing. They have held onto old wineskins, which become obstacles to God doing something new in them. They have confused tradition with the living Word of God.

This is an issue within the indigenous Latino Pentecostal evangelical church of which I have been a part for so many years. The Pentecostal evangelical church received the U.S. Latino community early on, particularly when other English-speaking churches were slow to respond to the growing numbers of Spanish-speaking arrivals to the country's shores. Particularly on the East Coast, an explosion of Pentecostal and evangelical churches embraced thousands of newly arrived people who thirsted for a personal relationship with Christ. Eventually, the dominant culture found it difficult to ignore the fact that Pentecostal churches were taking over buildings everywhere. Overnight, hundreds of churches were springing up everywhere, especially in Latino neighborhoods.

I, of course, owe my formation to the indigenous Pentecostal church.

It is where I first was discipled, trained for ministry, and ministered. Yet from the start I was aware that the indigenous church was falling into a trap similar to the one that caught the churches formed during God's previous activities in history. They believed the hype that their revelation from God was the fullness of his revelation. Progressive revelation had met its end in them. God had nothing more to teach them. In the early stages of my ministry, I wrestled with this belief. But I intuitively understood that we had more to learn from God. I felt that if we became closed to new revelations from God, the method by which God had lifted us up would become the means by which we would alienate and dominate other disenfranchised people. The oppressed would become the oppressors.

Regrettably, the status quo has prevailed to a large extent in the indigenous church. Over the decades I have witnessed many anointed men and women leave the movement in a mass exodus. The signs of religious captivity were evident and tangible. Many in my church were influenced by the liberation theology of Gustavo Gutiérrez and the progressive theology of Orlando Costas, and they sought to include those views in the movement. But many indigenous church leaders rejected these views and shunned any who sought so-called "external" and therefore ungodly sources of inspiration.

In many ways this could be characterized as a struggle between anti-intellectualism and intellectualism. It contributed to the emergence of post-denominationalism and triggered the rise of institutional religious networks and independent churches. Without a doubt, the indigenous Pentecostal church was a resource to many qualified leaders. But it also was slow to adapt God's dynamic activity in the movement. Their loss has become someone else's gain. The continuing "brain drain" threatens to impact future generations.

In spite of this, God is not through with the indigenous Pentecostal evangelical church. I accepted and made known God's progressive revelation in the spaces he saw fit to place me.[4] It happened in New York Theological Seminary, when I partnered with the late Rev. Dr. Bill Webber, the seminary president, to establish a college-seminary program for non-degree pastors, in conjunction with Adelphi University. It also happened with my partnering ministries of the LPAC National Urban Ministry Proj-

---

4. I have been moved by the view of Eldin Villafañe and others, who see the Pentecostal church as a signpost of God's Kingdom.

ect. I convinced the church to develop community-based ministries for the community at large. And it took place with the collective indigenous Pentecostal evangelical leadership, when I rallied them to protest the unfair treatment of immigrants, expanding their focus from the traditional issues of family values, same-sex marriage, and abortion. In these and other cases, I understood that I could be rejected. But I knew I was backed by the Word of God and the Holy Spirit. What I had to do was proclaim God's plan and purpose.

Test Movements of God and Embrace His Miraculous Signs

Of course, God focuses his people on matters that are consistent with his attributes and purpose. This is why he moved them to stand up for the abolition of slavery, for women's suffrage, for the rights of workers and immigrants and people of color, for the unborn, and for community service. At the same time, we also must test the spirit of the various movements we encounter, as they can appear to be, but at their essence are not, from God. Not all roads lead to Rome. There is evil in the world. Jesus warned us about false grace (Matthew 7:21-22), and the Word points to false prophets (Matthew 24:24; Mark 13:22). But we must be careful not to reject movements of God because we have unintentionally conformed to the world's lack of concern for the things of God. For instance, many churches have not shared God's concern for the poor and needy, who occupy a place of priority in God's Kingdom (Luke 12:32).

Another movement of God is immigration reform. While the public discourse has focused on the supposed negative financial impact of immigrants, I have sought to abide by Jesus' instruction in Matthew 25:35 to welcome the stranger. Jesus is clear that our failure to receive the stranger as one of the "least of these" — let alone tend to the hungry, thirsty, naked, sick, and imprisoned — is essentially the same as having rejected Jesus himself (25:42-46). The penalty for such inaction is eternal punishment.

God also promises that miraculous signs will follow his people (Luke 16:17-18). Such signs will lead others to believe (John 4:48). In today's society, people are suspicious when they hear about miracles. They often think of Moses parting the Red Sea, or Jesus raising Lazarus from the dead. To them, miracles cannot happen today, even if they may have happened in biblical times. Even in circles that accept miracles, such miracles often are relegated to special and select people.

When I think of God's miraculous signs, I think of the college program at New York Theological Seminary, which has since served as a prototype of seminary-undergraduate partnerships throughout the country and around the world. I also think of the gifting of LPAC's Urban Ministry Complex by the NYC Mission Society, the oldest private social services agency in New York City. After four years of success and growth as one of its divisions, Mission Society gifted LPAC its City Mission Cadet Corps building in the Highbridge neighborhood of the Bronx to serve as LPAC's headquarters. We paid a token ten dollars for the more than 40,000-square-foot building. Today it houses the K-8 Family Life Academy Charter School (FLACS) and several community organizations and churches.

At their essence, I view miracles as revealing a real authority born out of our transcendent vision and experience with God (Matthew 7:9). Indeed, your spirit and life bear witness to the people who are listening to you and seeing your work. People may not get it, but you act on your convictions, which are informed by your faith. Everyone may not agree with you, and you may even take risks. But this is all just part of your calling. If you are acting on your faith, you are able to do it. When the pressure comes, you do not succumb. Like David, you do not run away from the giant.

Early on in my ministry, I had an experience that reflects the authority I had in Christ. I was visiting distant cousins in Rochester, New York. They were practitioners of spiritualism, or *Espiritismo* as we say in Spanish. When I entered the house, the spiritual leader mentioned that I had a good spirit. As a result, they did not conduct the séance they had been planning to hold. They recognized that the Lord was with me. They discerned the calling on my life. I had grace with them (Acts 2:47). I did not have to say anything, but my spirit bore witness to the people there that their actions were not acceptable to God. At a basic level, I had inspired them to recognize God's authority.

I also remember the work I did with the participants of LPAC's TANF Program. After just one day, I noticed a sparkle in their eyes, a spring in their walk. Many seemed to believe again that change was possible. Not only were we in compliance with the NYC Human Resources Administration, but many who had abandoned hope and desire found it again. Even when we interacted with HRA, the personnel recognized our authority and treated our staff with respect. It was similar to when I successfully navigated the federal bureaucracy to launch the National Urban

Ministry Project, and the state education bureaucracy to launch FLACS. In each case, the powers recognized the authority of the church to serve the community, especially school-age children.

Recognize When God Is Calling You to a Transitional Role

Transitional figures are a built-in part of God's new movements, and there is always the possibility that he is calling you to be one. When God is set to alter the conditions of our reality, consistent with his purpose, those whom he calls have to straddle both the present and the future. In many ways, these individuals find themselves misunderstood and rejected by those who seek to preserve the status quo and who have ideas of a different future than the one they profess.

If God calls you to be a transitional person, you will be instrumental in bringing forth a new era in God's creation. Like John the Baptist, you will be part of the old ways, but you will operate out of a *kairos* moment, or a God-orchestrated time, and usher in a new set of conditions. Most likely you will feel isolated and lonely. You may even lack the necessary support, as it still may be emerging — given the newness of your message and call. Indeed, you may find yourself in the "desert" as you await the fulfillment of what is being birthed. As a result, you will have to discern the things that will drive you forward into the new era. Very likely you will have to contend with non-discerning members of the church and society, especially traditionalists and legalists. But remain faithful to God's call!

Ever since I began ministering at nineteen years old, I understood intuitively our collective call to repentance and renewal, and our citizenship in the Kingdom of God. Over the years I have been burdened to bring forth a holistic gospel that includes both personal piety and systemic engagement. As I revealed this message, many in the grassroots responded to the message, while many religious and political leaders opposed it. But I was faithful, and my faithfulness led to my successes. Some may suggest that the many challenges I faced are evidence that a holistic gospel is not God's plan for our time. I can only remind them that the success of God's people was not measured by their lack of adversity. As you may recall, John the Baptist was beheaded. Jesus was crucified. James, Peter, and Paul died martyrs. Rev. Dr. Martin Luther King Jr. was assassinated. Yet their successes led to the faithful ministries of future generations of God's people. This has motivated and compelled me to continue proclaiming the good news of holistic ministry.

Of course, transitions can be difficult for others to bear. In Ezra's time, the older generation, who remembered the building of the first temple, cried, while the new generation rejoiced at the sight of the second temple (Ezra 3:12). The elders recalled the beauty of the old temple that was no longer. Indeed, people often reminisce about the first works. But God's movement in history is continuous. He is always doing great things. Our glory is successive and progressive. We go from one glory to another, so we cannot get stuck on yesterday as God is working out our tomorrows.

Over the years I experienced my share of resistance to transition. At El Camino Pentecostal Church and Melrose Reformed Church, some balked at the idea of transition toward a holistic gospel and ministry. But I remained steadfast, and soon for the first time traditional evangelistic ministries and community ministries were operating side by side. Prayer was taking place in community activities. Community services were integrated into evangelistic activities. We were giving water in the name of Jesus.

I will not tell you that everyone stayed and accepted the transitions. But I discerned God's call to a holistic way of doing ministry, so I worked with those old and new who received the same holistic message. I also prayed for those who parted ways. Throughout, I accepted the hits I had to take for representing Christ inside and outside of the church. But during these and other transitions, I experienced Christ's faithfulness.

CHAPTER 9

A Final Word

So here you are, my fellow traveling companion on this journey to self-discovery and purpose. By now, I trust you have found that God is calling you to minister in a situation of captivity. You have connected to my ministry journey and have derived lessons and principles that you will be able to apply in your life and calling. Thus, you grasp what captivity means to our world, and you understand that you're not subject to that captivity. You are called to be free. I dare to believe that in the near future you will be confronting and engaging your own spiritual community, as well as the principalities and powers in your life and the society. In the process, you will be proclaiming the good news of personal and social transformation. Essentially, you will be working toward Jesus' prayer, *thy Kingdom come.*

I wish I can say that what I have brought you in this book is the alpha and omega, the beginning and the end. But I cannot. The journey continues. My ministry may have begun at nineteen years old and has continued past my sixty-fifth birthday, but I still have things to learn. I face challenges every day. I deal with paradox, bitterness, and indignations. At the same time, I still experience God's grace, love, and power. I believe you may experience trials but also will be blessed by Christ's gifts in your ministry.

In the end, Christ is sufficient. He makes us content in all things. So expect him to provide the resources you will need to be a blessing in the world around you. Believe that the circumstances you live in, or were shaped by, will not deter you from fulfilling the call upon your life. Ac-

159

cept that nothing can depart you from the love of God, his plan, his purpose, and your destiny. The generations that have come before you have had their Goliaths but also their Davids. You can be the David for your generation. Will you accept the challenge? I pray you do.